dYnamic ADOBE PHOTOSHOP GUIDE 2024

From Beginner to Pro | Unlocking the Secrets of Advanced Techniques for Breathtaking Visual Effects

WisdomBytes Solutions

Copyright © 2024 WisdomBytes Solutions
All rights reserved.

No portion of this book may be reproduced in any form without written permission from the publisher or author, except as permitted by U.S. copyright law.

This publication is designed to provide accurate and authoritative information in regard to the subject matter covered. It is sold with the understanding that neither the author nor the publisher is engaged in rendering legal, investment, accounting or other professional services. While the publisher and author have used their best efforts in preparing this book, they make no representations or warranties with respect to the accuracy or completeness of the contents of this book and specifically disclaim any implied warranties of merchantability or fitness for a particular purpose. No warranty may be created or extended by sales representatives or written sales materials. The advice and strategies contained herein may not be suitable for your situation. You should consult with a professional when appropriate. Neither the publisher nor the author shall be liable for any loss of profit or any other commercial damages, including but not limited to special, incidental, consequential, personal, or other damages.

TABLE OF CONTENTS

TABLE OF CONTENTS III

CHAPTER 1: INTRODUCTION TO ADOBE PHOTOSHOP 2024 1

Evolution of Photoshop: A Journey through Its Latest Iterations 2

Early Days and Pixel-Pioneering Efforts (1980s): 3
    The Rise of a Creative Powerhouse (1990s-Early 2000s) 3
    Continuous Innovation and The Future (2000s-Present): 4

1.2 Unveiling the Power of 2024: Exploring New Features and Enhancements 5
    Boosting Workflow and Efficiency: 5
    AI-Powered Smart Filters and Effects: 5

Generative Fill: 6
    Real-World Applications of New Features: 8
    A Glimpse into the Future: 8

1.3 Understanding the Symbiosis Between Traditional Editing and AI Integration 9
    Symbiosis in Action: The Perfect Blend 10
    The Takeaway: A Powerful Partnership 11

1.4 A Glance Through Your Creative Canvas: The Photoshop Workspace and Tools 11
    Understanding the Layout: 11
    Essential Tools for Everyday Editing: 12
    A Stepping Stone to Creative Exploration: 12

Summary 13

Review Questions 14

CHAPTER 2: ESSENTIAL TOOLS AND TECHNIQUES REFINEMENT 15
    Accessing Tools in Photoshop 2024: 16

2.1 Mastering the Essentials: Refining Your Editing Workflow 17

    Selection Tools Revisited: 17
    Advanced Cropping and Transformation Techniques: 20

2.2 Layer Management: Unleashing the Power of Non-Destructive Editing.23
    Understanding Layer Hierarchy: 24
    Leveraging Layers for Non-Destructive Editing: 24
    Mastering Blending Modes: 25

2.3 Advanced Color Correction and Color Space Management 26
    Beyond Basic Adjustments: 26
    Understanding Color Space: 27
    Color Profiles: 27

Summary 28

Review Questions 29

CHAPTER 3: UNDERSTANDING ARTIFICIAL INTELLIGENCE IN PHOTOSHOP 30

3.1 Demystifying AI: A Primer on its Role and Impact in Image Editing 31
    What is AI? 31
    AI in Image Editing Landscape 31
    Benefits of AI-powered Features 32
    Limitations of AI in Photoshop 33

3.2 Investigating the Neural Network Architecture behind AI-powered Features 33
    Understanding Neural Networks 34
    Different Types of Neural Networks in Photoshop 35
    How Neural Networks Learn 35

3.3 Application of AI in Automated Workflows and Predictive Editing 38
    1. AI-powered Selection Tools: 38
    3. Noise Reduction and Sharpening: 39
    4. Predictive Editing and Recommendations: 40
    Additional Considerations: 40

Summary 41

Review Questions 42

CHAPTER 4: ADVANCED SELECTION TECHNIQUES WITH AI INTEGRATION 43

4.1 Unraveling the Intricacies of AI-driven Selection Tools: A Deep Dive into Power and Potential 44

4.2 Exploring the Synergy Between Traditional and AI-based Selection Methodologies: A Marriage of Power and Precision 46

4.3 Case Studies and Practical Applications in Professional Editing Scenarios: Unleashing the Power in Real-World Projects 48
- Case Study 1: Effortless Portrait Selection with AI................................ 49
- Case Study 2: Clean Product Cutouts for E-commerce Success 50
- Case Study 3: Seamless Compositing with AI and Traditional Techniques 51

Summary 54

Review Questions 55

CHAPTER 5: CREATIVE IMAGE MANIPULATION WITH NEURAL FILTERS 56

5.1 Harnessing the Creative Potential of Neural Filters: A Guide to Artistic Exploration 57
- Understanding the Power of AI:.. 57
- Accessing the Neural Filters Gallery:... 57
- Exploring the Filter Categories and Previews:.. 57
- Unveiling the Power of Individual Filters:... 58
- Customizing Filter Effects (Optional):... 59

5.2 Exploring Innovative Approaches to Image Enhancement and Manipulation: A World of Creative Possibilities 60
- Case Study 1: Breathing New Life into Old Photos with Style Transfer 60
- Case Study 2: Transforming Landscapes with the Landscape Mixer 61
- Case Study 3: Color Grading with a Twist Using Color Transfer 61

Summary 62

Review Questions 63

CHAPTER 6: AI-POWERED CONTENT CREATION AND GENERATION 65

6.1 Exploring AI-driven Content Creation Tools and Capabilities 66
   6.1.1 Text Generation: Unveiling the Power of AI Writing Assistants................... 66
   6.1.2 Image and Video Generation: From Concept to Creation with AI 67
   6.1.3 Music Composition: AI-powered Melodies and Soundscapes 68

6.2 Understanding the Implications of AI-Generated Content in Digital Media 69
   6.2.1 Revolutionizing Workflows: Efficiency and Time-Saving Benefits 69
   6.2.2 Democratizing Content Creation: Accessibility and New Opportunities .. 69
   6.2.3 Evolving Consumer Expectations: The Future of Content Consumption .. 70

6.3 Ethical Considerations and Implications of AI-Generated Content Creation 71
   6.3.1 Ownership and Attribution: Who Owns AI-Generated Content?................ 71
   6.3.2 Bias and Fairness: Mitigating Algorithmic Bias in AI Content Creation 72
   6.3.3 Impact on Human Creativity: Collaboration or Competition?...................... 72

Summary 73

Review Questions 75

CHAPTER 7: ADVANCED RETOUCHING TECHNIQUES WITH AI ASSISTANCE 76

7.1 Mastering Advanced Retouching Techniques with AI-driven Tools in Photoshop 2024 77

7.2 Exploring AI-powered Skin Retouching and Texture Enhancements in Photoshop 2024 82

7.3 Ethical and Responsible Use of AI Retouching Tools 87

Summary 89

Review Questions 90

CHAPTER 8: STREAMLINING WORKFLOWS WITH AUTOMATION AND AI SCRIPTS 91

8.1 Harnessing the Power of Automation with Photoshop Scripts and Actions 91
   8.1.1 Understanding Scripts and Actions: Building Blocks of Automation 92
   8.1.2 Recording Your First Action: Capturing the Magic 93

8.1.3 Editing and Modifying Recorded Actions: Fine-tuning Your Automation 96
8.1.4 Batch Processing with Actions: Automating Edits for Multiple Images 98

8.2 Creating Custom AI-driven Scripts for Task Automation and Optimization 100
8.2.1 Introduction to Photoshop Scripting Languages 100
8.2.2 Creating Your First Script Using Actions: A Basic Tutorial for Automation in Photoshop 101
8.2.3 Integrating third-party AI tools and APIs for enhanced functionality 103

Summary 109

Review Questions 110

CHAPTER 9: INTEGRATING 3D AND AUGMENTED REALITY WITH PHOTOSHOP 111

9.1 Exploring the Convergence of 3D Modelling and Augmented Reality in Photoshop 112
9.1.1 Understanding 3D Integration 112
9.1.2 Demystifying Augmented Reality 113
9.1.3 The Power of Combining 3D and AR: Blurring the Lines Between Reality and Imagination 114

9.2 Creating Immersive AR Experiences with AI-powered Object Recognition 115
9.2.1 Leveraging AI for Object Recognition in Your Images 115
9.2.2 Building Interactive AR Experiences with Recognized Objects 116
9.2.3 Real-world Applications: Bringing AR Experiences to Life 117

9.3 Leveraging 3D and AR for Interactive Design and Storytelling 120
9.3.1 Enhanced Design Presentations: From Static to Immersive 120
9.3.2 Captivating Storytelling Techniques: Beyond the Page 121
9.3.3 The Future of Creative Expression: Boundless Potential 122

Summary 124

Review Questions 124

CHAPTER 10: DESIGNING FOR WEB AND MOBILE WITH AI INTEGRATION 125

10.1 Streamlining Responsive Design with AI: Unleashing the Power of AI-powered Layout Suggestions 126
    10.1.1 Unveiling the Magic of AI-powered Layout Suggestions 126
    10.1.2 Mastering Adaptive Design Techniques with AI Integration 128

10.2 User-Centered Design with AI: Unveiling User Behavior Through AI Analytics 130
    10.2.1 Integrating User Research with AI Analytics 130

10.3 Optimizing Design Workflows with AI 131
    10.3.1 Exploring AI Tools for Design Automation 131

10.4 The Future of AI-powered Web and Mobile Design 132
    10.4.1 Emerging AI Technologies for Design 133
    10.4.2 Ethical Considerations and Responsible Use of AI 133

CHAPTER 10 SUMMARY: UNLEASHING THE POWER OF AI FOR WEB AND MOBILE DESIGN 135

Review Questions 137

CHAPTER 11: MASTERING PHOTOSHOP 2024: ADVANCED TECHNIQUES AND BEST PRACTICES 138

11.1 Conquering the New Frontier: Exploring the Updated Photoshop Interface 139
    11.1.1 Navigating the Workspace in Photoshop 2024 140
    11.1.2 Crafting Your Ideal Workspace: A Guide to Customization in Photoshop 2024 142
    11.1.3 Mastering the Updated Toolbar in Photoshop 2024 with Powerful New Features 145
    11.2.2 Advanced Blending Modes: Unveiling the Magic of Layer Interactions 150
    11.2.3 Selective Adjustments and Masking: Unveiling the Art of Precise Editing 152

11.2.4 Content-Aware Tools: Unleashing the Power of AI-Assisted Editing 155

11.3 Professional Retouching: Unveiling the Secrets of the Masters 156

11.4 Compositing: Mastering the Art of Creating Surreal Imagery 159

11.5 Unleashing the Hidden Gems: Lesser-Known Features and Shortcuts in Photoshop 2024 161

11.6 Professional Editing Case Studies: Witnessing the Mastery in Action 162

Summary 164

Review Questions 164

CHAPTER 12: ADVANCED IMAGE EDITING TECHNIQUES: PUSHING THE BOUNDARIES 165

12.1.1 Frequency Separation Mastery: Refining Skin Texture Control 165
12.1.2 Advanced Dodge and Burn: Sculpting with Light and Shadow 166
12.1.3 Portrait Sculpting with Liquify: The Art of Subtlety 168

12.3 Complex Photo Manipulation and Compositing: Pushing the Boundaries of Reality 169

12.2.1 Advanced Selection and Masking Techniques: Precision is Key 169
12.2.2 Advanced Cloning and Healing: Seamless Integration 170
12.2.3 Advanced Compositing Workflows: Orchestrating Reality 171
Bringing the Extraordinary to Life 172
Refining Control with Advanced Masking 173
The Illusion of Movement with Matchmoving 175

12.3 Mastering Masking and Blending for Flawless Integration 176

12.3.1 Advanced Blending Modes and Adjustments: Pushing Creative Boundaries 176
12.3.2 Advanced Masking Workflows: Refining Control with Nested Masks ... 177

12.4 Color Grading and Tonal Adjustments: The Art of Professional Finishing 178

12.4.1 The Power of Color Grading: Setting the Mood 178
12.4.2 Tonal Adjustments: Refining Light and Shadow 179

12.5: Real-world examples and case studies showcasing the application of advanced editing skills 180

12.6.1 Case Study: Bringing a Travel Photo to Life 180
12.5.2 Sharpening Your Editing Eye: 182
Before & After: A Powerful Tool for Visual Learning 184
12.5.3 Learning from the Masters: Pro Insights on Advanced Editing 186

Summary 187

Review Questions 188

Conclusion: Beyond the Pixels of Photoshop 2024 188

INDEX 190

CHAPTER 1: INTRODUCTION TO ADOBE PHOTOSHOP 2024

Have you ever looked at a captivating photograph and wondered how it achieved such visual brilliance? Or perhaps you've dreamt of creating your own stunning imagery, but felt intimidated by complex editing software. Well, fret no more! Adobe Photoshop 2024 is here to empower you on your creative journey.

This comprehensive guide serves as your gateway to mastering this industry-standard software. Whether you're a seasoned photographer, a budding graphic designer, or simply an enthusiast with an eye for beauty, Photoshop 2024 offers a treasure trove of tools and techniques to unlock your creative potential.

Throughout this chapter, we'll embark on a fascinating exploration:

A Legacy of Innovation: We'll delve into the rich history of Photoshop, tracing its evolution from its early days to its current position as the leading image editing software.

- **Unveiling the Power of 2024:** We'll dive deep into the exciting new features and interface enhancements introduced in Photoshop 2024.
- **Tradition Meets Innovation:** We'll explore the harmonious blend of traditional editing tools and cutting-edge AI integration within Photoshop 2024.
- **Navigating Your Creative Canvas:** We'll take a guided tour of the user interface, familiarizing you with the essential tools and panels that will become your creative companions within Photoshop.

By the end of this chapter, you'll be well-equipped with the foundational knowledge to begin your exciting adventure with Adobe Photoshop 2024. Let's get started!

Evolution of Photoshop: A Journey through Its Latest Iterations

Welcome to the fascinating world of Adobe Photoshop! This section takes you on a captivating journey through the history of this industry-standard software, from its humble beginnings to its current status as a powerhouse for image editing.

Early Days and Pixel-Pioneering Efforts (1980s):

- Our story starts in the mid-1980s, with two brothers, Thomas and John Knoll, at the helm. Back then, personal computers were still in their early stages, and image editing software was a niche concept.
- Thomas, a Ph.D. student in computer science, was passionate about photography and frustrated by the limitations of editing grayscale images on his monochrome Macintosh Plus display. This frustration sparked the creation of a program called "Display," the very first iteration of what would eventually become Photoshop.
- John, working in the film industry with Industrial Light & Magic, saw the potential of his brother's creation. Together, they embarked on a journey to refine and expand the capabilities of "Display," eventually adding features like layers, selections, and basic tonal adjustments.
- In 1988, after striking a licensing deal with Adobe Systems Incorporated, the first commercial version of Photoshop was released for Macintosh computers. This initial version offered a limited but groundbreaking set of tools, forever changing the landscape of digital image editing.

The Rise of a Creative Powerhouse (1990s-Early 2000s)

- The 1990s witnessed the meteoric rise of Photoshop. With each new release, the software's feature set grew exponentially, attracting a broader audience beyond just professional photographers.
- Key milestones during this period include:
    - Introduction of filters, a powerful toolset for adding creative effects and artistic transformations to images.
    - Implementation of channels, allowing for precise control over color information within an image.
    - Development of masking techniques, enabling users to selectively edit specific areas of an image while preserving others.

- - Introduction of non-destructive editing tools, a revolutionary concept that allowed for editing adjustments without permanently altering the original image file.
- As Photoshop became more user-friendly and affordable, it empowered a new generation of creative individuals. Graphic designers embraced its capabilities for creating stunning visuals for print and web. Hobbyist photographers explored its potential to enhance and transform their captured moments.
- The impact of Photoshop transcended the realm of software – it became a cultural phenomenon. Its influence could be seen in graphic design trends, web design aesthetics, and even the way we perceive and interact with digital imagery.

Continuous Innovation and The Future (2000s-Present):

- The early 2000s saw further advancements in Photoshop, solidifying its position as the undisputed leader in image editing software. Features like layer effects, advanced selection tools, and content-aware healing capabilities offered even greater creative control and editing finesse.
- Today, Adobe Photoshop continues to push the boundaries of what's possible. The 2024 iteration boasts cutting-edge features powered by artificial intelligence (AI). Imagine using AI-powered tools to:
  - Intelligently generate content that seamlessly blends into existing images.
  - Significantly improve image quality, especially in low-light photographs, with AI-powered noise reduction.
  - Effortlessly select complex objects or regions within an image with the help of machine learning algorithms.
- As you delve deeper into the world of Photoshop 2024, you'll experience firsthand the culmination of this remarkable evolution. The powerful tools and innovative features at your disposal will

empower you to create and transform images in ways never before possible.

This section has provided a glimpse into the remarkable journey of Photoshop. Understanding its rich history and ongoing development allows you to appreciate the capabilities of this software and the exciting creative possibilities that lie ahead in Photoshop 2024.

1.2 Unveiling the Power of 2024: Exploring New Features and Enhancements

The latest iteration of Photoshop, 2024, brings a wave of exciting new features and interface enhancements designed to elevate your image editing experience. Get ready to explore functionalities that empower you to work with greater efficiency and unleash your creative potential.

Boosting Workflow and Efficiency:

- **Enhanced Core Functionalities:** Imagine refined selection tools with improved edge detection for precise object isolation. Streamlined layer organization options will help you maintain control even in complex compositions. Content-aware features, like the ever-popular Content-Aware Fill, might receive further refinements for seamless content replacement and background generation.
- **AI-Powered Assistants:** A significant focus of Photoshop 2024 is the integration of artificial intelligence (AI) into the editing workflow. Here are some game-changers:

AI-Powered Smart Filters and Effects:

1. **What are They?**
    - **Smart Filters and Effects** in Photoshop 2024 leverage AI to adapt intelligently to the content of your image.

- These features analyze the image and adjust their parameters to complement specific characteristics, resulting in enhanced visual effects.

2. **How to Access Them:**
   - To use **Smart Filters and Effects**:
     - Navigate to the **Filter** menu.
     - Choose **Neural Filters**.
     - Explore the available filters under **All Filters**.
     - Some filters may need to be downloaded from the cloud before first use (indicated by a cloud icon).
     - Enable and adjust the filter settings in the panel on the right.
     - Note that portrait-related filters will be grayed out if no faces are detected in the image.

3. **Use Cases**:
   - Apply stylized effects, enhance textures, or add dynamic lighting.
   - These filters adapt to your image content, making your editing process more efficient.

Generative Fill:

1. **What is Generative Fill?**
   - **Generative Fill** is a powerful feature in Photoshop 2024.
   - It allows you to effortlessly fill, edit, or remove image elements using machine learning AI.
   - The tool generates new contextual pixels that may not exist in the original image.
   - It's non-destructive, allowing easy reversion of changes.

2. **Accessing Generative Fill:**

3. To use **Generative Fill**:
    - Select an area using any selection tool.
    - Click the **Generative Fill button** in the **Contextual Task Bar**.
    - Provide a prompt describing the object or scene you want to generate (or leave it blank for automatic context-based filling).
4. **Use Cases**:
    - Extend images.
    - Generate backgrounds.
    - Create realistic objects.
    - Remove or replace elements.
    - Compose unique composite images.
5. **Tips for Generative Fill**:
    - Leave the prompt blank for creative surprises.
    - Experiment with different selections.
    - Avoid instructional prompts.
    - Blend photos together using this feature.

- **Customizable Workspace:** Photoshop 2024 prioritizes user comfort. The interface might offer more options for customization, allowing you to arrange panels and tools in a way that best suits your editing style. Additionally, keyboard shortcuts can be personalized to streamline your workflow and maximize efficiency.

Real-World Applications of New Features:

These advancements translate into tangible benefits for various creative fields:

- **Photographers:** AI noise reduction can breathe new life into photos taken in challenging lighting conditions. Content-Aware Fill can assist in removing unwanted objects or blemishes with ease.
- **Graphic Designers:** Generative Fill can be a powerful tool for creating unique and eye-catching backgrounds for layouts and presentations. Smart selection tools can expedite the process of isolating intricate design elements.
- **Web Designers:** Improved selection tools can aid in precise image manipulation for web layouts, ensuring pixel-perfect integration of visual elements within web pages.

A Glimpse into the Future:

By understanding these new features and their potential applications, you'll be well-equipped to harness the power of Photoshop 2024. This software continuously evolves, and the future holds the promise of even more groundbreaking innovations that will redefine the boundaries of image editing. As you embark on your creative journey with Photoshop, remember that exploration and experimentation are key to unlocking your full artistic potential.

1.3 Understanding the Symbiosis Between Traditional Editing and AI Integration

The magic of Photoshop 2024 lies in the harmonious blend of traditional editing tools and cutting-edge AI integration. This section explores how these two seemingly disparate forces work together to empower your creative vision.

Traditional Editing Tools: The Foundation of Your Workflow

- At the heart of Photoshop lies a robust set of tried-and-true editing tools that have formed the bedrock of image editing for decades. These tools provide you with granular control over every aspect of your image, from basic adjustments like exposure and color correction to advanced techniques like masking and compositing.
- A foundational understanding of these tools remains paramount. Mastering tools like:
    - **Selection tools:** These allow you to isolate specific areas of your image for targeted editing. From the classic Lasso tool to the more advanced Pen tool, mastering selection techniques is a crucial skill.
    - **Adjustment layers:** These offer a non-destructive way to fine-tune aspects like brightness, contrast, hue, and saturation. They allow for experimentation and easy adjustments without altering the original image data.
    - **Layers and blending modes:** Layers provide a hierarchical structure for organizing your edits. Blending modes determine how underlying layers interact with each other, creating a vast array of creative effects.
- By honing your skills with these traditional tools, you gain a deeper understanding of the image editing process itself. This foundation allows you to leverage the power of AI features more effectively.

AI Integration: A Creative Powerhouse at Your Fingertips

While traditional tools provide control, AI integration in Photoshop 2024 injects a dose of intelligent automation and creative exploration. Imagine these possibilities:

- **Effortless Object Removal:** Imagine using a content-aware tool powered by AI to remove unwanted objects from your image with surprising accuracy. This could be a game-changer for photographers or graphic designers who need to clean up their compositions.
- **AI-Assisted Compositing:** Creating fantastical scenes that blend real-world elements with imaginative objects can be time-consuming. AI-powered tools might assist in seamlessly integrating 3D elements or generating realistic lighting effects within your compositions.
- **Intelligent Color Grading:** Color grading plays a crucial role in setting the mood and evoking emotions within your viewers. New AI features might analyze your image and suggest color palettes or adjustments that complement the overall composition.

Symbiosis in Action: The Perfect Blend

The true power of Photoshop 2024 lies in understanding how traditional tools and AI features work together. Don't view AI as a replacement; instead, see it as a collaborator that can enhance your workflow and amplify your creative vision.

- **AI can expedite tedious tasks:** Imagine using AI to generate a rough mask around a complex object, and then refining it with traditional tools for ultimate precision.
- **AI can spark new creative ideas:** Let's say you're unsure about the color palette for your image. AI suggestions can serve as a starting

point for exploration, ultimately leading you to a unique and personalized color grading choice.

The Takeaway: A Powerful Partnership

By embracing both traditional and AI-powered tools, you unlock the full potential of Photoshop 2024. Remember, AI is a powerful assistant, not a replacement for your creative decision-making. As you gain experience, you'll develop an intuitive understanding of how to leverage both approaches to achieve stunning and impactful results in your image editing projects.

1.4 A Glance Through Your Creative Canvas: The Photoshop Workspace and Tools

Welcome to your creative playground! This section offers a guided tour of the Photoshop 2024 user interface, equipping you with the foundational knowledge to navigate its vast array of tools and panels.

Understanding the Layout:

- Imagine Photoshop 2024 as a customizable workspace. The interface consists of several key areas:
    - **Document Window:** This is the central area where your image is displayed. You can zoom in and out to view specific details or get a full overview of your composition.
    - **Menu Bar:** Located at the top of the screen, the menu bar provides access to various functions categorized by menus like "File," "Edit," "Image," and "Filter."
    - **Tool Panels:** Docked along the left side of the workspace, these panels house all the essential editing tools, categorized by function (e.g., Selection tools, Adjustment tools, Painting tools).

- **Panels:** These customizable panels (like Layers, Channels, History) offer additional functionalities and information about your image. You can arrange them to suit your workflow preferences.
- **Properties Bar:** Located at the top of the workspace, this context-sensitive bar displays options and controls specific to the currently selected tool.

Essential Tools for Everyday Editing:

While Photoshop boasts a comprehensive set of tools, here's a quick introduction to some essentials for common editing tasks:

- **Selection Tools:** These allow you to isolate specific areas of your image for targeted editing. The Lasso tool lets you draw a freehand selection, while the Rectangular Marquee tool creates precise squares or rectangles.
- **Adjustment Tools:** Fine-tune the overall look and feel of your image with tools like Levels (for brightness and contrast), Curves (for advanced tonal adjustments), and Hue/Saturation (for color correction).
- **Healing and Cloning Tools:** Remove unwanted blemishes or imperfections using the Spot Healing Brush or Patch Tool. These tools intelligently sample surrounding areas to seamlessly fill in unwanted elements.
- **Dodge and Burn Tools:** Lighten or darken specific areas of your image for localized adjustments. These tools are perfect for adding depth, dimension, and subtle lighting effects.

A Stepping Stone to Creative Exploration:

This brief overview equips you with the basic navigation skills to explore the vast potential of Photoshop's tools and panels. Remember, this is just the first step on your creative journey. As you delve deeper into the software, you'll discover a treasure trove of functionalities waiting to be explored. Don't be afraid to experiment, try new tools, and customize your workspace to suit your editing style.

The more you practice, the more comfortable you'll become navigating the Photoshop interface and wielding its powerful tools to create stunning and impactful imagery.

Summary

This first chapter of "Mastering Photo Editing with Adobe Photoshop 2024" serves as an introduction to the software's rich history, exciting new features, and core functionalities.

A Legacy of Innovation: We explored Photoshop's evolution, from its humble beginnings to its current status as the industry standard for image editing. We discussed its impact on various creative fields like photography and graphic design.

Unveiling the Power of 2024: This section delved into the latest features and interface enhancements of Photoshop 2024. We explored how these features, such as AI-powered content creation and noise reduction, empower users to edit images with greater efficiency and unleash their creative potential.

Symbiosis of Tradition and Innovation: The chapter emphasizes the harmonious collaboration between traditional editing tools and AI integration within Photoshop 2024. We discussed how AI complements existing workflows without replacing them, allowing for a powerful and creative partnership.

A Glance Through Your Creative Canvas: Finally, we embarked on a guided tour of the Photoshop 2024 user interface. This section provided a basic understanding of the layout, essential tools for common editing tasks, and how to navigate the workspace for a smooth and efficient editing experience.

This knowledge of Photoshop 2024's history, functionalities, and user interface equips you to start your creative journey in the realm of image editing.

Review Questions

1. Briefly describe the evolution of Adobe Photoshop, highlighting its transition from its early days to its current position as the leading image editing software.
2. Explain the concept of symbiosis between traditional editing tools and AI integration within Photoshop 2024. Discuss how AI features can enhance, rather than replace, your creative workflow in image editing.
3. Imagine you're working on a photograph with unwanted elements in the background. Describe two or three tools available in the Photoshop 2024 workspace that you could potentially use to address this issue, and explain how they function differently.

CHAPTER 2: ESSENTIAL TOOLS AND TECHNIQUES REFINEMENT

Welcome back to your journey into the world of Photoshop 2024! Chapter 1 provided a solid foundation, introducing you to the software's history, exciting new features, and the user interface. Now, it's time to refine your editing skills and unlock the full potential of this powerful software.

This chapter delves into the essential tools and techniques that form the backbone of image editing in Photoshop 2024. We'll revisit familiar tools like selection, cropping, and transformation, but this time with a focus on their advanced functionalities and the refinements introduced in the latest version.

Imagine achieving precise object selections with improved edge detection, or seamlessly manipulating image perspective with content-aware cropping suggestions. These are just a few of the exciting possibilities that await you in this chapter.

But our exploration doesn't stop there. We'll also embark on a deep dive into layer management, a core concept in Photoshop. Layers provide a non-destructive editing environment, allowing you to make adjustments to specific image components without altering the original data. By mastering the art of layering and leveraging enhanced blending modes, you'll be able to create stunning visual effects and composite elements with ease.

Finally, the chapter equips you with advanced color adjustment techniques and proper color space management. Moving beyond basic adjustments like brightness and contrast, you'll learn how to manipulate specific color ranges and ensure accurate color representation throughout your editing workflow.

Accessing Tools in Photoshop 2024:

Before we delve into specifics, let's take a moment to familiarize ourselves with how to access the tools we'll be discussing. The essential tools for selection, cropping, and transformation are all conveniently located within the **Tools Panel** on the left side of the Photoshop workspace.

- **Selection Tools**

- Look for icons like the rectangular marquee tool (looks like a dotted rectangle), the lasso tool (looks like a loop), and the Pen tool (looks like a curved pen).
- **Cropping Tool:** This is represented by a cropping tool icon (looks like a rectangle with corner handles).
- **Transformation Tools:** These are located under the Edit menu at the top of the screen. Look for options like "Free Transform" (Ctrl/Cmd + T) and "Perspective Warp."

Layers and their associated functionalities can be accessed through the **Layers Panel,** typically located on the right side of the workspace. Blending modes are available within the drop-down menu next to each layer in the Layers Panel.

Color adjustment tools can be found in several locations. Basic adjustments like Levels and Curves can be accessed through the **Image** menu at the top of the screen. More specific color correction tools like Selective Color and Hue/Saturation can be found under the **Adjustments** menu within the same Image menu.

With this roadmap in mind, let's begin our journey to mastering essential tools and techniques in Photoshop 2024! Get ready to refine your editing skills and unlock the full creative potential of this software.

2.1 Mastering the Essentials: Refining Your Editing Workflow

Now that you're familiar with where to find the tools, let's dive deeper into mastering essential techniques in Photoshop 2024. This section focuses on refining your workflow with selection tools, cropping, and transformation functionalities.

Selection Tools Revisited:

We'll revisit three fundamental selection tools: the Lasso Tool, the Rectangular Marquee Tool, and the Pen Tool. While you might be familiar with their basic functionalities, Photoshop 2024 offers some exciting refinements to enhance precision and control.

- **Lasso Tool (Freehand Selection):** This classic tool allows you to draw a freehand selection around an object. In 2024, the Lasso tool boasts improved edge detection. Here's how to use it:

1. Select the Lasso tool from the Tools Panel.
2. Click anywhere on the edge of your object and begin dragging your mouse to create a selection outline.
3. As you move your mouse, the improved edge detection helps the tool "stick" to the object's edges, creating a more precise selection.
4. Once you've traced around the entire object, release the mouse button.
5. (Optional) Refine your selection by using the "Refine Edge" option in the top toolbar. This allows you to adjust feathering for smoother edges or contract/expand the selection for greater precision.

- **Rectangular Marquee Tool (Square/Rectangular Selections):** Ideal for selecting straight-edged objects. 2024 offers the option to constrain the selection to a perfect square or specific aspect ratio while using this tool. Here's how:

1. Select the Rectangular Marquee tool from the Tools Panel.
2. Hold down the "Shift" key while dragging your mouse to create a perfect square selection.
3. Hold down the "Alt" key (Option key on Mac) while dragging to open a menu where you can specify a desired aspect ratio (e.g., 16:9 for widescreen format).
4. Drag the marquee tool to encompass the desired area of your image.

- **Pen Tool (Precise Path Selection):** For intricate selections with curves or specific shapes, the Pen tool offers unparalleled control. Here's a basic introduction:
    1. Select the Pen tool from the Tools Panel.
    2. Click at a starting point on the outline of your object. This creates an anchor point.
    3. Click again at another point along the outline. A straight line segment is created between the two points.

4. To create a curve, click and hold at a point, and then drag your mouse slightly away from the line path. This creates a direction handle for the curve. Release the mouse button to set the curve.
5. Continue clicking and dragging to create additional anchor points and curves, following the outline of your object.
6. Once you've traced the entire object, click back on the first anchor point (indicated by a small circle) to complete the path. This creates a closed selection.

These are just the fundamentals, and with practice, you'll master these tools for creating precise selections in your images.

Advanced Cropping and Transformation Techniques:

Move beyond basic cropping with the tools available in Photoshop 2024.

- **Content-Aware Cropping:** Imagine cropping an image and having the background intelligently filled based on the surrounding content! This is possible with the Content-Aware Crop option.
    1. Select the Crop tool from the Tools Panel.

2. Drag the crop handles to define your desired framing.
3. In the Options bar at the top, look for the checkbox labeled "Content-Aware." Tick this box.
4. As you move the crop handles, Photoshop will use AI to analyze the surrounding content and suggest a natural-looking fill for the cropped area.

- **Aspect Ratio Constrain:** Maintain specific aspect ratios while cropping with this handy feature.
    1. Select the Crop tool.

2. In the Options bar, look for the drop-down menu next to "W:" (width). Here, you'll find options for pre-defined aspect ratios like "Original," "16:9," or "4:3." Select your desired ratio.

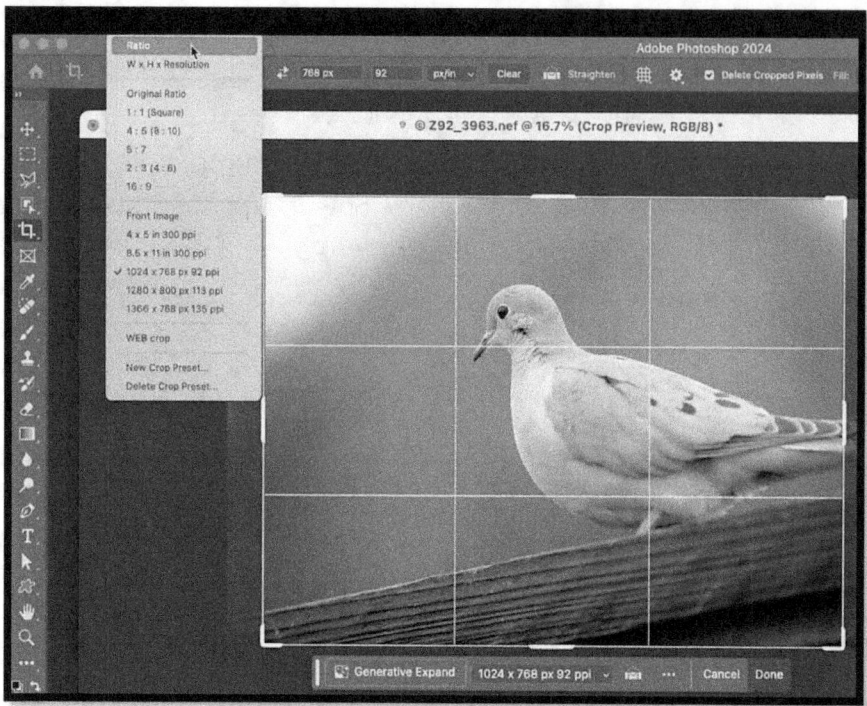

3. Cropping your image will now maintain the chosen aspect ratio.
- **Advanced Transformations:** Go beyond simple scaling and rotating with the powerful transformation tools in Photoshop 2024.
    1. Select the layer you want to transform (usually the background layer for overall image adjustments).
    2. Go to the Edit menu at the top of the screen. Here, you'll find a variety of transformation options:

    Free Transform (Ctrl/Cmd + T): This allows you to resize, rotate, skew, and distort your image non-destructively. Drag the corner handles to resize, hold down "Shift" while dragging to constrain proportions, or hold down "Ctrl" (Cmd on Mac) while dragging to distort the image. * **Perspective Warp (Edit > Transform > Perspective Warp):** This powerful tool allows you to adjust the perspective of your image. Imagine correcting a photo where buildings appear to be leaning due to the camera angle. Click and drag the corner handles of the grid overlay to manipulate the perspective and achieve a more natural look.

Efficiency Boosters:

While mastering these tools is essential, efficiency is key in a creative workflow. Here are some tips to streamline your selection and transformation processes:

- **Feathering and Anti-aliasing:** For smoother selections that blend seamlessly into the background, utilize the feathering option in the top toolbar when using the Lasso tool or creating selections with the Pen tool. Anti-aliasing further refines the edges of your selection to prevent jagged pixels, especially important for text or vector elements.
- **Keyboard Shortcuts:** Photoshop offers a vast array of keyboard shortcuts for various tools and functionalities. Learning these shortcuts can significantly speed up your editing workflow. Explore the Edit menu and other menus to discover available shortcuts or customize your own in the Keyboard Shortcuts preferences.

Mastering these refined selection, cropping, and transformation techniques grants you greater control and precision while editing your images in Photoshop 2024. The next section will delve into the world of layer management, a powerful concept that unlocks a whole new level of creative freedom within your editing workflow.

2.2 Layer Management: Unleashing the Power of Non-Destructive Editing

Layers are the foundation of non-destructive editing, allowing you to make adjustments to specific image components without altering the original data. Imagine editing text on a poster without affecting the background image – that's the magic of layers!

Understanding Layer Hierarchy:

The Layers Panel, typically located on the right side of the Photoshop workspace, displays a hierarchical structure of your image. By default, a new image starts with a single layer called "Background." As you edit your image and add elements, new layers are created. Here's a breakdown of some key layer concepts:

- **Background Layer:** This layer contains the original image data. In Photoshop 2024, you can convert the background layer into a regular editable layer for more flexibility.
- **New Layers:** Whenever you use a tool like the Paint Brush or add text, a new layer is created. This allows you to edit or hide these elements independently without affecting underlying layers.
- **Layer Opacity and Blending Mode:** Each layer has an opacity slider that controls its visibility. A layer at 100% opacity is fully visible, while a layer with lower opacity becomes partially transparent. Blending modes, accessible through the drop-down menu next to each layer, determine how the layer interacts with the layers below it. We'll explore blending modes in more detail in the next section.

Leveraging Layers for Non-Destructive Editing:

Layers empower you to experiment and refine your edits without jeopardizing the original image. Here are some practical examples:

- **Color Correction on a Separate Layer:** Imagine adjusting the color balance of your image. Instead of directly editing the background layer, you can create a new "Curves" adjustment layer. This allows you to fine-tune the colors without affecting the underlying image data. If you don't like the adjustment, you can simply delete the Curves layer and start again.
- **Adding Text with Flexibility:** Adding text directly to the background layer makes it difficult to edit later. Instead, create a

new text layer for your text elements. This allows you to change the font, size, or position of the text without affecting the rest of your image.

Mastering Blending Modes:

Blending modes are a powerful toolset within layer management. They define how the colors in a layer interact with the colors in the layers below it. Here's a glimpse into some popular blending modes and their effects:

- **Normal:** This is the default mode, where the layer appears exactly as it is.
- **Multiply:** Darkens the underlying layers based on the darkness of the pixels in the current layer. Great for adding shadows or creating a darkening effect.
- **Screen:** Lightens the underlying layers based on the lightness of the pixels in the current layer. Useful for creating light leaks or adding a glowing effect.
- **Overlay:** Creates a contrast effect based on the pixel values in the current layer. Darker pixels become darker, and lighter pixels become lighter in relation to the underlying layers.

Experimenting with different blending modes can unlock a vast array of creative possibilities for compositing elements, adding textures, and achieving unique visual effects within your images.

Beyond the Basics:

This section has provided a foundational understanding of layer management in Photoshop 2024. As you progress, you'll discover even more advanced layer functionalities like layer masks, clipping masks, and adjustment layer properties. These tools offer even greater control and flexibility within your non-destructive editing workflow.

2.3 Advanced Color Correction and Color Space Management

Color plays a crucial role in conveying emotions, setting the mood, and guiding the viewer's eye within your image. This section equips you with advanced color correction techniques and proper color space management for optimal image manipulation in Photoshop 2024.

Beyond Basic Adjustments:

We'll move beyond simple tools like Brightness/Contrast and explore more advanced functionalities for precise color manipulation.

- **Selective Color:** This powerful tool allows you to target specific color ranges within your image and adjust them independently. Imagine selectively adjusting the red tones in your image to enhance the vibrancy of a flower while leaving other colors untouched. Access Selective Color through the **Adjustments** menu within the **Image** menu at the top of the screen.
    1. Go to Image > Adjustments > Selective Color.
    2. The Selective Color window displays various color dropdowns like "Reds," "Yellows," "Magentas," etc. Select the color range you want to adjust.
    3. Use the sliders for "Neutrals," "Cyans," "Magentas," "Yellows," and "Blacks" to fine-tune the specific color range. For example, increasing the "Magentas" in the "Reds" dropdown might enhance the vibrancy of red flowers.
- **Hue/Saturation Adjustment:** This tool allows you to globally adjust the hue (color itself), saturation (intensity of the color), and lightness of all colors within your image. While this can be a powerful tool, use it subtly to avoid oversaturated or unrealistic colors. Access Hue/Saturation Adjustment similar to Selective Color (Image > Adjustments > Hue/Saturation).

- **Color Balance:** This tool lets you adjust the balance between the highlights, midtones, and shadows within your image in terms of red, green, and blue (RGB) color channels. Imagine correcting a scene with a strong yellow cast by reducing the yellow levels in the highlights or shadows. Find Color Balance under the same Adjustments menu (Image > Adjustments > Color Balance).

Understanding Color Space:

The concept of color space refers to the range of colors a device can display or an image file can store. Understanding color space is crucial for maintaining consistent color representation throughout your editing workflow and for final output.

- **RGB vs. CMYK:** Most digital images use the RGB (Red, Green, Blue) color space, which is ideal for screen display. However, the printing industry relies on CMYK (Cyan, Magenta, Yellow, Black) color space. It's important to convert your image to CMYK before sending it to print to ensure accurate color reproduction. You can find the color space options under the **Image** menu at the top of the screen (Image > Mode > CMYK Color).
- **Monitor Calibration:** A well-calibrated monitor is essential for ensuring that the colors you see on your screen accurately represent the actual colors in your image. Uncalibrated monitors can display colors with a bias, leading to inaccurate editing decisions. Consider investing in a monitor calibration tool to ensure consistent color representation throughout your workflow.

Color Profiles:

Color profiles are sets of data that define how a device interprets and displays colors. Using the correct color profile for your monitor and printer helps maintain consistent color accuracy. Photoshop 2024 allows you to assign and manage color profiles within the **Edit** menu at the top of the screen (Edit > Assign Profile).

By mastering these advanced color correction techniques and maintaining proper color space management, you'll ensure that your images boast optimal visual quality and consistent color representation across various mediums.

Summary

This chapter, "Essential Tools and Techniques Refinement," focused on equipping you with the skills to elevate your image editing workflow in Photoshop 2024. We revisited fundamental tools like selection (Lasso, Rectangular Marquee, Pen), cropping, and transformation, exploring their advanced functionalities and refinements in the latest version.

Selection Mastery: Improved edge detection in the Lasso tool and the ability to constrain aspect ratios while cropping empower you to make precise selections for targeted edits.

Transformation Techniques: Move beyond basic scaling and explore content-aware cropping suggestions, aspect ratio constraints, and advanced tools like perspective warp for manipulating image perspective with greater control.

Unlocking the Power of Layers: We delved into the concept of layer management, the foundation of non-destructive editing. Layers allow you to make independent adjustments to specific image components without altering the original data. Understanding layer hierarchy, opacity, and blending modes empowers you to experiment creatively and refine your edits with flexibility.

Advanced Color Correction: Beyond basic adjustments like brightness/contrast, we explored powerful tools like Selective Color,

Hue/Saturation Adjustment, and Color Balance for precise manipulation of specific color ranges within your image.

Color Space Management: Maintaining accurate color representation throughout your workflow is crucial. This section discussed the difference between RGB and CMYK color spaces, the importance of monitor calibration, and how to manage color profiles for consistent color output.

These essential tools and techniques, sets the foundation to create high-quality, visually impactful images in Photoshop 2024. Remember, consistent practice is key to refining your editing skills and unlocking the full creative potential of this powerful software.

Review Questions

1. Describe two improvements introduced in Photoshop 2024 for the Lasso selection tool and explain how they can enhance the precision of your selections.
2. Non-destructive editing is a cornerstone of working with layers in Photoshop. Explain the concept of layer hierarchy and how it allows you to make adjustments to specific image elements without affecting the underlying image data.
3. Differentiate between RGB and CMYK color spaces. When would you use each, and why is proper color space management essential in image editing?

CHAPTER 3: UNDERSTANDING ARTIFICIAL INTELLIGENCE IN PHOTOSHOP

Welcome to the exciting frontier of image editing – the realm of Artificial Intelligence (AI)! Photoshop 2024 has embraced AI technology, transforming the way we create and manipulate images. This chapter delves into the fascinating world of AI within Photoshop, demystifying its role and showcasing its profound impact.

Whether you're a seasoned Photoshop user or just starting your journey, AI offers a multitude of benefits. Imagine effortlessly selecting complex objects, breathing life into dull photos with intelligent noise reduction, or receiving personalized suggestions for edits based on your image content. AI streamlines workflows, enhances accuracy, and unlocks new creative possibilities.

But before we dive into the wonders of AI-powered features, let's take a step back. This chapter will begin by providing a foundational understanding of AI itself. We'll explore basic concepts like machine learning and deep learning, shedding light on how machines can "learn" and perform tasks that were once considered the exclusive domain of human intelligence.

Next, we'll delve into the fascinating world of neural networks – the architecture that powers AI within Photoshop. Imagine a complex web of interconnected nodes, inspired by the human brain, that can analyze and process information. We'll explore different types of neural networks used in Photoshop and how they are trained on massive datasets of images to perform specific tasks.

Finally, we'll get hands-on! We'll explore how AI is revolutionizing everyday workflows in Photoshop. From the magic of AI-powered selection tools to the power of content-aware fill and healing brush, we'll showcase how AI automates tedious tasks and empowers you to focus on your creative vision. We'll also explore the future of Photoshop with AI, teasing the potential of predictive editing and personalized recommendations.

This chapter is your gateway to understanding and utilizing the power of AI in Photoshop. Get ready to unlock a world of efficiency, accuracy, and boundless creative possibilities!

3.1 Demystifying AI: A Primer on its Role and Impact in Image Editing

This section breaks down the core concepts of Artificial Intelligence (AI) and its impact on the landscape of image editing in Photoshop 2024.

What is AI?

Artificial intelligence refers to the ability of machines to mimic human cognitive functions, such as learning and problem-solving. Machine learning, a subfield of AI, empowers machines to improve their performance on a specific task without explicit programming. This is achieved by training them on vast amounts of data, allowing them to identify patterns and make predictions.

Deep learning, a more advanced form of machine learning, utilizes artificial neural networks – complex algorithms loosely inspired by the structure and function of the human brain. These neural networks consist of interconnected nodes that process information in layers, gradually learning and refining their ability to perform tasks.

AI in Image Editing Landscape

The integration of AI in Photoshop has significantly transformed the image editing experience. Here's how:

- **Accessibility:** AI automates complex tasks, making Photoshop more approachable for users of all experience levels. Repetitive actions become effortless, freeing up time for creative exploration.
- **Efficiency:** AI streamlines workflows by automating tedious tasks like background removal or noise reduction. This allows you to focus on more creative aspects of image editing.
- **Accuracy:** AI-powered features deliver superior results compared to traditional methods. For instance, AI can perform more precise object selections or noise reduction with minimal image artifacts.
- **Creative Exploration:** AI opens doors to new creative possibilities. Imagine experimenting with AI-powered filters that adapt to your image content or receiving suggestions for edits that enhance your creative vision.

However, it's important to remember that AI is still under development. While it excels at specific tasks, human expertise remains crucial for creative decision-making and handling complex scenarios.

Benefits of AI-powered Features

Let's delve deeper into the specific advantages of AI in Photoshop:

- **Automation:** AI automates repetitive tasks, saving you time and effort. Imagine effortlessly selecting a person in a busy background using the "Select Subject" tool, or removing unwanted objects with the "Content-Aware Fill" powered by AI.
- **Improved Accuracy:** AI-powered features often deliver superior accuracy compared to traditional methods. For example, AI can remove noise from an image while preserving fine details, or perform object selections with remarkable precision.
- **Enhanced User Experience:** AI personalizes the Photoshop experience. Imagine receiving content-aware suggestions for edits or filters based on your image content, or having the software recommend actions based on your editing history.

Limitations of AI in Photoshop

While AI offers significant benefits, it's essential to acknowledge its limitations:

- **Human Expertise Still Matters:** AI excels at specific tasks but cannot replicate human creativity and judgment. The success of an image edit often hinges on the user's artistic vision and ability to make creative decisions.
- **Potential for Bias:** AI algorithms are trained on massive datasets of images. If these datasets contain biases, the AI may perpetuate those biases in its outputs. It's crucial to be aware of this potential limitation and use AI tools with a critical eye.
- **Evolving Technology:** AI is a rapidly evolving field. While AI-powered features in Photoshop are impressive, they are constantly being improved and refined.

By understanding both the strengths and limitations of AI, you can leverage its power to enhance your workflow and unleash your creative potential in Photoshop.

3.2 Investigating the Neural Network Architecture behind AI-powered Features

This section delves into the intricate architecture that powers AI within Photoshop. Imagine a complex web of interconnected nodes, inspired by the human brain, that can analyze and process information with remarkable capabilities. Here, we'll explore how these neural networks function and how they are harnessed to deliver the magic of AI-powered features in Photoshop.

Understanding Neural Networks

Neural networks are a type of artificial intelligence algorithm loosely inspired by the structure and function of the human brain. They consist of interconnected nodes, often called artificial neurons, arranged in layers. Each layer receives information from the previous layer, processes it using a specific mathematical function, and then transmits the processed information to the next layer.

Here's a breakdown of the key components of a neural network:

- **Artificial Neurons:** These are the building blocks of a neural network, mimicking the function of neurons in the human brain. They receive input signals, apply mathematical functions (activation functions), and generate an output signal.
- **Layers:** Neural networks are typically organized into multiple layers, with each layer performing a specific transformation on the data. The first layer receives the raw input data (e.g., an image), and subsequent layers progressively extract more complex features from the data.
- **Connections:** The power of neural networks lies in the connections between neurons. These connections have associated weights, which determine the influence of one neuron on another. By adjusting these weights during the training process, the network learns to identify patterns and relationships within the data.
- **Training:** Neural networks don't possess inherent knowledge. They learn through a process called training, where they are exposed to vast amounts of labeled data. For example, in Photoshop, a neural network used for content-aware fill might be trained on millions of images with corresponding information about object removal and background replacement. Through this training, the network learns to identify patterns and relationships within the data, enabling it to perform similar tasks on new, unseen images.

Different Types of Neural Networks in Photoshop

While there are many types of neural networks, Photoshop primarily utilizes two architectures:

- **Convolutional Neural Networks (CNNs):** These are particularly adept at image recognition and analysis tasks. CNNs consist of alternating convolutional layers and pooling layers. Convolutional layers extract features from the image, such as edges, shapes, and textures. Pooling layers then downsample the data, reducing its dimensionality while preserving important features. By stacking these layers, CNNs can learn increasingly complex representations of the image, allowing them to perform tasks like object classification, image segmentation (separating objects from the background), and noise reduction.
- **Generative Adversarial Networks (GANs):** These are a more recent development in the field of AI. GANs consist of two competing neural networks: a generator and a discriminator. The generator network attempts to create new, realistic images, while the discriminator network tries to distinguish between real images and the generated ones. Through this adversarial process, both networks improve their capabilities. While not as widely used in Photoshop 2024 as CNNs, GANs have the potential to revolutionize tasks like image inpainting (filling in missing image regions) and style transfer (applying the artistic style of one image to another).

How Neural Networks Learn

As mentioned earlier, neural networks learn through a process called training. This involves feeding the network massive amounts of labeled data relevant to the task at hand. For instance, training a neural network for content-aware fill might involve showing it countless images with corresponding information about the objects to be removed and the desired background replacements.

Here's a simplified breakdown of the training process:

1. **Data Preparation:** The first step involves preparing a large dataset of labeled images. These images are carefully curated to ensure they represent the variety of situations the network might encounter in real-world use.
2. **Forward Pass:** During training, an image from the dataset is fed into the neural network layer by layer. Each layer performs its specific function, transforming the data and extracting relevant features.
3. **Error Calculation:** The network's output is then compared to the desired outcome (the labeled data). The difference between the network's prediction and the actual outcome is calculated as an error.
4. **Backpropagation:** This is the heart of the learning process. The calculated error is propagated backward through the network, adjusting the weights of the connections between neurons. These adjustments aim to minimize the error in future predictions.
5. **Iteration:** Steps 2-4 are repeated numerous times, iterating through the entire training dataset. With each iteration, the network progressively refines its weights, becoming better at identifying patterns and relationships within the data

The training process is iterative, meaning the network goes through the data set multiple times. With each iteration, the error between the network's prediction and the actual outcome gets smaller, signifying that the network is learning and improving its ability to perform the task.

There are several factors that influence the effectiveness of training a neural network:

- **Data Quality and Quantity:** The quality and quantity of training data are paramount. High-quality, well-labeled data that encompasses the range of scenarios the network might encounter in real-world use is crucial for optimal performance. A limited dataset or data with inconsistencies can lead to biases or inaccuracies in the network's outputs.

- **Network Architecture:** The specific architecture of the neural network, including the number of layers, the type of neurons used, and the connections between them, all play a role in its learning capabilities. Choosing the right architecture for the task at hand is essential for achieving optimal results.
- **Training Parameters:** The training process involves various parameters that can be fine-tuned to optimize learning. These include the learning rate, which controls how much the network adjusts its weights with each iteration, and the number of training epochs (complete passes through the data set). Finding the right balance for these parameters is crucial for efficient training and avoiding issues like overfitting (where the network memorizes the training data but fails to generalize to unseen examples).

Once a neural network is trained, it can be used to make predictions on new, unseen data. In the context of Photoshop, this translates to applying AI-powered features to your images. For instance, a trained neural network can analyze an image to identify objects for selection, perform content-aware fill to seamlessly remove unwanted elements, or reduce noise while preserving image details.

While the inner workings of neural networks can be complex, understanding the basic principles behind them empowers you to appreciate the power of AI in Photoshop. As AI technology continues to evolve, we can expect even more sophisticated and creative applications of neural networks within the software, further transforming the landscape of image editing.

3.3 Application of AI in Automated Workflows and Predictive Editing

AI has revolutionized workflows in Photoshop by automating repetitive tasks and introducing intelligent features that streamline the editing process. Let's delve into some of the key areas where AI shines in Photoshop 2.4:

1. AI-powered Selection Tools:

- **Select Subject:** This intelligent tool leverages AI (specifically CNNs) to analyze your image and automatically select the main subject, separating it from the background with impressive accuracy. This eliminates the tedious process of manual selection with tools like lassos or magic wands, especially for complex objects with intricate details like hair or fur.
- **Object Selection Tool:** Building upon the power of Select Subject, this tool allows you to refine the selection further. Using AI, you can select specific objects within the image by simply brushing over them. The AI analyzes the object's characteristics like color, texture, and depth, and creates a precise selection, saving you time and effort.

2. Content-Aware Fill and Healing Brush:

- **Content-Aware Fill:** This powerful tool utilizes AI to seamlessly remove unwanted objects from your image. Simply select the object and hit delete. The AI analyzes the surrounding image content and intelligently generates pixels to fill the gap, creating a natural-looking result. This is particularly helpful for removing blemishes, power lines, or distracting elements from your photos.
- **Healing Brush:** Similar to Content-Aware Fill, the Healing Brush allows you to remove imperfections or unwanted details. By brushing over the area you want to fix, the AI analyzes the surrounding texture and patterns and replaces the unwanted element with a more natural-looking patch.

3. Noise Reduction and Sharpening:

- **Noise Reduction:** Digital photos often suffer from noise, which appears as unwanted grain or speckles. AI-powered noise reduction tools in Photoshop analyze the image and differentiate between actual image details and noise artifacts. The AI then selectively reduces the noise while preserving the sharpness and clarity of the image.

- **Sharpening:** Sharpening an image enhances its detail and crispness. AI-powered sharpening tools go beyond traditional methods by analyzing the image content and applying localized sharpening adjustments. This ensures that edges are sharpened without creating halos or unnatural artifacts.

4. Predictive Editing and Recommendations:

While still under development, AI has the potential to revolutionize image editing with features like predictive editing and recommendations. Imagine AI analyzing your image and suggesting content-aware fill options, recommending specific filters or adjustments based on the image content, or even proposing creative edits that enhance your photo's overall impact. These features are still in their early stages, but they offer a glimpse into the exciting future of AI-powered image editing.

Additional Considerations:

- **System Requirements and Hardware Acceleration:** Utilizing AI features in Photoshop can be demanding on your computer's resources. For optimal performance, ensure you have a system that meets the recommended specifications for Photoshop, particularly a powerful graphics card (GPU) that can accelerate AI computations. Many AI features in Photoshop leverage GPUs for faster processing.
- **Ethical Considerations of AI:** As with any AI technology, it's important to be mindful of potential biases. AI algorithms are trained on vast datasets of images, and if these datasets contain biases, the AI may perpetuate those biases in its outputs. It's crucial to be aware of this limitation and use AI tools with a critical eye. For instance, if an AI content-aware fill tool is primarily trained on images of landscapes, it might struggle to seamlessly fill in missing elements in a portrait due to a lack of relevant training data.

By understanding the applications of AI in Photoshop, you can leverage its power to streamline your workflow, achieve superior editing results, and unlock new creative possibilities. As AI technology continues to evolve, we can expect even more groundbreaking features that will transform the way we edit images in Photoshop.

Summary

This chapter has unveiled the fascinating world of Artificial Intelligence (AI) within Photoshop 2024. We've explored how AI is revolutionizing image editing, automating tasks, enhancing accuracy, and opening doors to new creative possibilities.

From the magic of AI-powered selection tools to the seamless content-aware fill and the intelligent noise reduction features, AI streamlines your workflow and empowers you to focus on the creative aspects of image editing. We've also peeked into the future with the potential of predictive editing and personalized recommendations, hinting at a future where AI becomes an even more collaborative partner in the creative process.

While AI offers undeniable benefits, it's important to remember that it's a tool, and like any tool, it requires a skilled user to wield it effectively. Understanding the limitations of AI and approaching it with a critical eye is crucial.

As you embark on your journey with AI-powered features in Photoshop, embrace the potential for exploration and experimentation. Don't be afraid to push the boundaries and see what creative results you can achieve. Remember, AI is here to assist you, not replace you. Your artistic vision and creative decisions will always be the driving force behind your edits.

The future of image editing is bright with AI. By harnessing its power and understanding its potential, you can elevate your skills and create stunning visuals in Photoshop 2024.

Review Questions

1. Explain the core concept of machine learning and how it empowers AI-powered features in Photoshop.
2. Compare and contrast two AI-powered selection tools in Photoshop (e.g., Select Subject and Object Selection Tool). Discuss their functionalities and potential benefits for image editing tasks.
3. AI has revolutionized image editing workflows in various ways. Describe two specific areas where AI excels in Photoshop, and explain how these features enhance the editing process.

CHAPTER 4: ADVANCED SELECTION TECHNIQUES WITH AI INTEGRATION

This chapter dives deep into the world of advanced selection techniques in Photoshop 2024. Our focus is on the powerful capabilities of AI-powered selection tools and how they can revolutionize your workflow. We'll explore how these tools work and how you can leverage them to achieve precise and efficient selections in your image editing projects.

However, tradition has its place! We won't neglect the importance of established selection methods in Photoshop. This chapter explores the synergy between AI and classic tools. By understanding the strengths of each approach, you'll be able to make informed decisions and achieve superior control over your selections.

Here's a roadmap for this chapter:

- **Unraveling AI Selection Tools:** Section 4.1 delves into the inner workings of these tools. We'll explore the technology behind them, specifically convolutional neural networks (CNNs), and how they analyze images to identify objects and create clean selections.
- **Beyond Automation:** Section 4.2 goes beyond simply using AI for automation. We'll explore how to leverage traditional selection methods like the Lasso Tool and Quick Selection Tool in conjunction with AI for optimal results. Understanding the strengths of both methodologies empowers you to make informed choices for your editing needs.
- **Real-World Applications:** Theory is valuable, but putting it into practice is essential! Section 4.3 showcases practical applications through compelling case studies. See how professional editors utilize advanced selection techniques, including AI integration, to achieve stunning results. We'll explore real-world scenarios like

isolating a product from a busy background or seamlessly compositing elements from different images.

By the end of this chapter, you'll be equipped with the knowledge and skills to master selection techniques in Photoshop 2024. You'll not only understand the power of AI-powered tools but also appreciate the enduring value of traditional methods. Get ready to unlock a world of creative possibilities and elevate your image editing to the next level!

4.1 Unraveling the Intricacies of AI-driven Selection Tools: A Deep Dive into Power and Potential

This section peels back the curtain, unveiling the fascinating inner workings of these tools and empowering you to harness their power for superior selection results in your image editing endeavors.

At the core of this revolution lies a sophisticated technology known as convolutional neural networks (CNNs). Imagine a complex web of interconnected nodes, inspired by the structure and function of the human brain. These nodes, called artificial neurons, process information in a layered fashion, progressively extracting meaningful features from the data they receive. In the context of selection tools, CNNs are trained on massive datasets of images. These datasets contain not only the images themselves, but also corresponding information about object boundaries and desired selections. Through this rigorous training process, the network learns to identify patterns and relationships within the data, developing the remarkable ability to recognize objects in new, unseen images.

Here's a deeper dive into the key functionalities of AI-driven selection tools, equipping you to leverage their capabilities for precise and efficient selections:

- **Object Recognition: The Power of AI-powered Identification**

One of the most transformative features of AI in selection is its object recognition prowess. Unlike traditional selection methods that rely on manual input or color similarity, AI-powered tools can intelligently identify and differentiate between various objects within an image. This translates to effortless selection of complex objects like people (even with flowing hair or intricate clothing), animals in motion, or specific elements within a busy scene. Imagine the time saved compared to meticulously outlining objects with tools like the Lasso Tool! With AI, selecting a person in a portrait becomes as simple as a single click, freeing you to focus on the creative aspects of your edit.

- **Background Segmentation: Isolating Objects with Precision**

Isolating objects from their backgrounds is a fundamental aspect of image editing, and achieving clean, precise selections is crucial for a professional outcome. AI excels at distinguishing between foreground objects and the background. This background segmentation capability empowers you to create clean selections around objects, perfect for tasks like:

* **Product Cutouts:** Effortlessly isolate a product from its cluttered background for e-commerce websites or marketing materials. No more painstakingly erasing unwanted background elements by hand!
* **Removing Distracting Elements:** Say goodbye to unwanted photobombers or distracting objects in your photos. AI can precisely select and remove these elements, leaving you with a clean and focused image.
* **Creating Composite Images:** Isolating objects with clean selections is a critical first step in creating captivating composite images. Imagine seamlessly integrating a person from one photo into a different background for a creative artistic effect.

- **Edge Detection: Achieving Flawless Precision**

The accuracy of a selection often hinges on precise edge detection, especially for objects with intricate details like hair, fur, or feathers. Traditional selection methods can struggle with these complexities, often resulting in jagged edges or unwanted halo effects. AI-powered selection tools, however, excel at detecting the edges of objects with remarkable precision. This ensures that your selections are clean and seamless, eliminating the need for tedious manual adjustments with tools like the Refine Edge brush. Fine details are preserved, and you achieve professional-looking results with minimal effort.

Understanding the core functionalities of AI-driven selection tools equips you to leverage their power and achieve superior results in your image editing projects. The next section will explore how these AI tools can be combined with traditional selection methods in Photoshop for an even more optimized workflow. We'll delve into the strengths of both approaches, empowering you to make informed decisions and achieve the most precise and efficient selections for your specific editing needs.

4.2 Exploring the Synergy Between Traditional and AI-based Selection Methodologies: A Marriage of Power and Precision

While AI-powered selection tools offer a revolutionary approach to image editing, the value of traditional selection methods in Photoshop shouldn't be underestimated. This section explores the importance of these classic tools and how they can be combined with AI for an optimized workflow that leverages the strengths of both approaches.

Traditional Selection Methods: A Legacy of Control

Photoshop offers a robust toolbox of traditional selection methods, each with its own strengths and weaknesses. Understanding these tools empowers you to make informed decisions and strategically combine them with AI for optimal results:

- **Lasso Tool: The Freehand Artist's Ally**

The Lasso Tool provides the freedom to freehand draw a selection around an object. This approach offers unparalleled control for complex shapes or intricate details that might challenge AI tools. Imagine carefully outlining the flowing hair of a portrait subject or the delicate fur of an animal – the Lasso Tool empowers you to achieve precise results. However, this method can be time-consuming for simple shapes or large areas.

- **Quick Selection Tool: Leveraging Color and Tone**

The Quick Selection Tool utilizes color and tonal similarities within an image to create selections. This method is efficient for selecting areas with consistent color, such as a blue sky or a solid-colored object. It can be a good starting point for AI tools to refine further. For instance, you might use the Quick Selection Tool to create a rough outline of a red flower, and then use an AI-powered tool like "Refine Edge" to perfect the selection around the delicate flower petals. However, the Quick Selection Tool can struggle with complex objects that have variations in color or intricate details.

- **Magic Wand Tool: A Speedy Selection for Uniform Colors**

The Magic Wand Tool excels at selecting areas based on similar color values. This method is incredibly fast for selecting solid-colored objects or backgrounds with minimal variations in tone. Imagine quickly selecting a bright red car against a blue sky. However, the Magic Wand Tool can struggle with objects that have even slight color variations or intricate details. It's not ideal for complex selections.

The Power of Synergy: Combining AI and Traditional Methods

The key to unlocking the full potential of selection techniques lies in understanding the strengths and weaknesses of both traditional and AI-based methods. By strategically combining them, you can achieve the most precise and efficient selections for your specific editing needs:

- **AI for Initial Selection, Traditional Tools for Refinement:** Leverage AI tools for their object recognition and background segmentation capabilities to create a fast and accurate initial selection. Then, utilize traditional tools like the Lasso Tool or Refine Edge brush for fine-tuning and achieving pixel-perfect precision around complex edges or intricate details.
- **Traditional Tools for Specific Needs, AI for Overall Refinement:** For simple shapes or color-based selections, traditional methods like the Quick Selection Tool or Magic Wand Tool can be efficient starting points. Then, refine the selection further using AI-powered tools like "Select Subject" or "Refine Edge" to ensure clean and seamless edges.

By understanding the complementary nature of traditional and AI-based selection methodologies, you can elevate your workflow and achieve professional-looking results in your image editing projects. The next section will showcase real-world examples of how professional editors leverage this synergy to tackle various editing challenges. We'll delve into practical applications of advanced selection techniques, including AI integration, to empower you to master these powerful tools in Photoshop 2024.

4.3 Case Studies and Practical Applications in Professional Editing Scenarios: Unleashing the Power in Real-World Projects

The world of professional image editing thrives on efficiency and precision. This section dives into the practical applications of advanced selection techniques, including AI integration, showcasing how these tools are utilized in real-world editing scenarios. Through compelling case studies, you'll witness firsthand how professional editors leverage this powerful combination to achieve stunning and impactful results.

Case Study 1: Effortless Portrait Selection with AI

Imagine the challenge of editing a portrait photograph with a person having flowing hair or wispy clothing. Traditionally, meticulously outlining the person using the Lasso Tool could be a time-consuming task. Here's how AI streamlines the process, with step-by-step instructions:

1. **AI to the Rescue:**
    - Open your portrait image in Photoshop 2024.
    - Go to the "Select" menu in the top bar.
    - Navigate down to the submenu and choose "Select Subject."

Photoshop's AI analyzes the image and automatically creates a selection around the person in the portrait. This selection often captures even the intricate details of the hair and clothing, significantly reducing editing time.

2. **Refinement for Perfection:**

While AI excels at initial selections, achieving pixel-perfect precision might require some refinement. Here's how to ensure a clean and natural separation from the background:

- In the Layers panel (usually on the right side of the workspace), click on the "Select Subject" layer thumbnail to activate the selection.
- Look for the "Refine Edge" button in the top Options bar. This button appears next to the selection mode dropdown (usually set to "Marching Ants"). Click on the "Refine Edge" button.

The Refine Edge workspace opens, offering various tools and settings to adjust the selection. Here are some key steps for refining hair selections:

* **View Mode:** Choose "Hair" from the View Mode dropdown menu. This optimizes the preview for fine details like hair strands.
* **Edge Detection:** If the automatic edge detection isn't perfect, use the "Refine Edge Brush" to paint over the hair strands. Refine the selection by adding hair strands to the selection (painting with white) or removing background pixels (painting with black). Adjust the brush size and feather settings for optimal control.
* **Output:** Choose "New layer with mask" from the Output To dropdown menu. This creates a new layer with a mask that precisely isolates the person from the background.

Case Study 2: Clean Product Cutouts for E-commerce Success

Product photography for e-commerce websites demands clean and professional-looking product cutouts. Here's how AI tackles this challenge, with a detailed walkthrough:

1. **Background Removal with AI:**
    - Open your product image in Photoshop 2024.
    - There are two primary AI-powered selection tools you can use:
        - **Select Subject:** This tool works well for products with distinct shapes and clear separation from the background. Go to the "Select" menu, navigate to the submenu, and choose "Select Subject."
        - **Object Selection Tool:** This tool offers more granular control for complex product shapes or cluttered backgrounds. In the Tools panel (usually on the left side of the workspace), click and hold on the Lasso Tool icon. A menu appears – choose "Object Selection Tool." Click and drag around the product to create a rough outline. Refine the selection using the on-screen handles and adjustment sliders.

The chosen AI tool analyzes the image and distinguishes the product from the background, creating a clean preliminary selection.

2. **Traditional Tools for Final Touches:**

While AI excels at background segmentation, there might be minor imperfections around the product edges. Here's how to achieve a flawless cutout with a clean, transparent background:

- In the Layers panel, click on the selection thumbnail (it might be named "Object Selection" or "Select Subject"). This activates the selection.
- Look for the "Refine Edge" button in the top Options bar and click on it.
- If there are small areas around the product edges that are still part of the selection (indicated by a red overlay in the Refine Edge workspace), use the "Refine Edge Brush" (paint with black) to remove them from the selection.
- Click "OK" to exit the Refine Edge workspace.
- In the Layers panel, click on the "Add Layer Mask" button at the bottom of the panel (a rectangle with a minus sign). This creates a mask that hides the background, effectively creating a clean product cutout.

Case Study 3: Seamless Compositing with AI and Traditional Techniques

Compositing images involves combining elements from different photos to create a new, imaginative scene. Here's how AI and traditional methods work together, with a step-by-step guide:

1. **AI for Initial Object Selection:**
    - **Preparing the Source Images:** Open the two images you want to use for your composite in separate Photoshop 2024

documents. Ensure the images have similar lighting and resolution for a more natural-looking final composite.
    - **Selecting the Object in the First Image:**
        - Identify the object you want to extract from the first image (e.g., a person from a portrait).
        - There are two main AI-powered selection tools you can use, depending on the object's complexity:
            - **Select Subject:** This tool works well for people, animals, or objects with distinct shapes. Go to the "Select" menu, navigate to the submenu, and choose "Select Subject."
            - **Object Selection Tool:** This tool offers more control for complex objects or backgrounds with clutter. In the Tools panel, click and hold on the Lasso Tool icon and choose "Object Selection Tool." Create a rough outline around the object and refine the selection using the on-screen handles and adjustment sliders.
- **Refining the Selection (Optional):** While AI does a good job initially, you might want to refine the selection for better control. Follow the steps mentioned in Case Study 1, Section 2 (Refinement for Perfection) to achieve a clean selection around the object using the Refine Edge brush.
- **Copying the Selected Object:** Once you're happy with the selection, press **Ctrl+C (Win) / Command+C (Mac)** to copy the selected object.

2. **Traditional Tools for Integration and Refinement:**
    - **Opening the Background Image:** Navigate to the document containing the background image for your composite and ensure it's the active window.

- **Pasting the Copied Object:** Press **Ctrl+V (Win) / Command+V (Mac)** to paste the copied object onto the background image as a new layer.
- **Positioning and Scaling:** Use the Move Tool (shortcut key **V**) to position the object in your desired location within the background scene. Freely transform the object's size and orientation using the Free Transform Tool (shortcut key **Ctrl+T (Win) / Command+T (Mac)**). Hold **Shift** while transforming to maintain the object's aspect ratio.
- **Masking for Seamless Blending (Optional):** For a more natural-looking composite, you can use Layer Masks to blend the object seamlessly into the background. Here's a basic masking workflow:
    - With the object layer selected in the Layers panel, click on the "Add Layer Mask" button at the bottom of the panel. This creates a black mask that hides the entire object.
    - Select the Brush Tool (shortcut key **B**) and choose a soft-edged white brush. Adjust the brush size and opacity to your liking.
    - Paint on the black mask to reveal the object in areas where you want it to blend naturally with the background. For instance, you might paint along the object's edges to soften them and create a gradual transition into the background.
- **Layer Blending Modes (Optional):** Experiment with different Layer Blending Modes (found in the dropdown menu at the top of the Layers panel) to further enhance the realism of your composite. Some common modes for compositing include "Multiply" for placing objects in shadows or "Overlay" for adding contrast and depth.

By following these steps and understanding the strengths of both AI and traditional selection techniques, you can create stunning and professional-looking composite images in Photoshop 2024. Remember, practice and experimentation are key to mastering these techniques and achieving your creative vision.

Summary

This chapter has unveiled the exciting world of advanced selection techniques in Photoshop 2024. We've delved into the transformative power of AI-powered selection tools, exploring how they revolutionize the way you isolate objects in your image editing projects. From effortless object recognition to precise background segmentation, AI streamlines your workflow and empowers you to achieve remarkable results with minimal effort.

However, the value of traditional selection methods shouldn't be overlooked. The Lasso Tool, Quick Selection Tool, and Magic Wand Tool each offer unique strengths and functionalities. Understanding these tools and how they can be strategically combined with AI empowers you to make informed decisions and achieve superior control over your selections.

The real magic lies in the synergy between AI and traditional methods. By leveraging AI for its initial selection capabilities and then utilizing traditional tools for refinement, you unlock the potential for pixel-perfect precision and professional-looking results. The case studies showcased in this chapter serve as practical examples, demonstrating how professional editors harness this combined power to tackle various editing challenges.

As you embark on your journey of mastering selection techniques, remember that practice is key. Experiment with the different tools and functionalities explored in this chapter. Don't be afraid to combine AI and traditional methods to see what works best for your specific editing needs. With dedication and exploration, you'll transform your image editing workflow, achieving superior efficiency, precision, and creative freedom in Photoshop 2024.

This chapter has equipped you with the knowledge and skills to take your selection techniques to the next level. Now, go forth and unlock the boundless creative possibilities that await you in the world of image editing!

Review Questions

1. When selecting a complex object with intricate details (like hair or fur) in Photoshop 2024, should you rely solely on AI-powered selection tools, or is there a benefit to combining them with traditional methods like the Refine Edge brush? Explain your answer.
2. Imagine you're creating a composite image in Photoshop 2024. In what order would you typically use AI-powered selection tools and traditional selection methods? Justify your workflow explanation.
3. Beyond the tools covered in this chapter, what other factors do you consider important for achieving clean and precise selections in Photoshop 2024?

CHAPTER 5: CREATIVE IMAGE MANIPULATION WITH NEURAL FILTERS

Welcome to the thrilling realm of creative image manipulation with Neural Filters in Photoshop 2024! This chapter unlocks a treasure trove of possibilities, empowering you to push the boundaries of image editing and transform your photos into captivating works of art.

We'll delve into the exciting world of Neural Filters, a powerful technology that leverages artificial intelligence (AI) to create stunning and often unexpected effects. Imagine transforming a portrait into a captivating watercolor painting or imbuing a landscape with the dreamlike quality of an impressionist masterpiece. With Neural Filters, these creative explorations become a reality within Photoshop 2024.

This chapter is segmented into two key sections:

- **Harnessing the Creative Potential of Neural Filters:** Section 5.1 equips you with a comprehensive understanding of Neural Filters. We'll explore their capabilities, functionalities, and the various artistic styles they offer. You'll learn how to navigate the Neural Filters interface and unleash your creative vision.
- **Exploring Innovative Approaches to Image Enhancement and Manipulation:** Section 5.2 delves into the practical applications of Neural Filters. We'll showcase inspiring case studies that demonstrate how professional editors leverage these filters to achieve transformative results. From subtle image enhancements to dramatic artistic transformations, you'll witness the power of Neural Filters in action.

By the end of this chapter, you'll be equipped with the knowledge and skills to utilize Neural Filters effectively in your image editing workflow. Get ready to unleash your creativity and explore a world of artistic possibilities in Photoshop 2024!

5.1 Harnessing the Creative Potential of Neural Filters: A Guide to Artistic Exploration

Neural Filters in Photoshop 2024 represent a paradigm shift in image editing, offering a gateway to a world of artistic exploration. This section delves into the core functionalities of these filters, empowering you to understand their capabilities and unleash your creative vision.

Understanding the Power of AI:

At the heart of Neural Filters lies artificial intelligence (AI), specifically a form of AI known as deep learning. Deep learning algorithms are trained on massive amounts of data, in this case, vast collections of images and corresponding artistic styles. Through this training, the AI learns to recognize patterns and relationships within the data, allowing it to apply artistic styles to new, unseen images.

Accessing the Neural Filters Gallery:

Here's how to access and navigate the inspiring Neural Filters Gallery in Photoshop 2024:

1. **Open the Filter Menu:** Go to the top menu bar and click on "Filter."
2. **Navigate to Neural Filters:** Within the dropdown menu under "Filter," scroll down and select "Neural Filters." This action launches the dedicated workspace for Neural Filters.

Exploring the Filter Categories and Previews:

The Neural Filters Gallery serves as your creative playground within Photoshop 2024. Here's a breakdown of its key functionalities:

- **Filter Categories:** On the left-hand side of the workspace, you'll find a panel displaying various filter categories. These categories are conveniently grouped to organize the diverse collection of filters and effects offered by Neural Filters. Some popular categories include:
    - **Style Transfer:** Apply artistic styles from various art movements or contemporary trends.
    - **Landscape Mixer:** Blend skies and atmospheric elements from different landscapes.
    - **Color Transfer:** Match the color palette and mood of a reference image.
    - **Depth Effects:** Generate realistic depth-of-field effects or enhance existing blur in your image.
    - **Super Resolution:** Enlarge your image size while preserving detail and sharpness.
- **Filter Previews:** Clicking on a specific filter within a chosen category displays a preview of its effect on your image in the large central workspace. This allows you to experiment with different filters and visualize the potential outcomes before applying them definitively. Hovering your cursor over a filter name might also display a brief description of the effect.

Unveiling the Power of Individual Filters:

Let's delve into some of the most popular and transformative Neural Filters in Photoshop 2024:

- **Style Transfer:** Imagine transforming your portrait into a captivating Van Gogh masterpiece or imbuing your landscape photo with the dreamlike quality of an impressionist painting. Style Transfer filters empower you to achieve these artistic transformations with a single click. Explore a variety of styles, from

classic art movements like pointillism and cubism to contemporary artistic trends.
- **Landscape Mixer:** Ever wondered what your beach scene would look like under a vibrant sunset from a different location? The Landscape Mixer allows you to seamlessly blend the sky and atmospheric elements from one landscape photo into another, creating breathtaking and imaginative composite images.
- **Color Transfer:** Breathe new life into your photos by transferring the color palette from a reference image. This filter allows you to match the mood and style of another image, infusing your photo with a specific color harmony or dramatic lighting effect.

Customizing Filter Effects (Optional):

While Neural Filters offer a wide range of preset effects, you're not limited to simply applying them with a single click. Many filters provide customization options that empower you to fine-tune the outcome and achieve the exact artistic vision you have in mind. These adjustments might be found within a panel on the right side of the workspace and might include sliders for controlling:

- The intensity of the filter effect.
- Specific style elements within a style transfer (e.g., brushstroke size or color emphasis).
- Masking options to selectively apply the filter to certain areas of your image.

Understanding the core functionalities of Neural Filters and exploring the creative possibilities within the Neural Filters Gallery puts you well on your way to unlocking a world of artistic exploration in Photoshop 2024. The next section delves into inspiring case studies, showcasing how professional editors leverage these powerful tools to achieve transformative results.

5.2 Exploring Innovative Approaches to Image Enhancement and Manipulation: A World of Creative Possibilities

The true power of Neural Filters lies in their ability to transform your images and push the boundaries of creativity. This section dives into inspiring case studies that showcase how professional editors leverage these filters to achieve stunning and unique results.

Case Study 1: Breathing New Life into Old Photos with Style Transfer

Imagine a faded family portrait from a bygone era. While the photo holds sentimental value, its age and condition might detract from its visual appeal. Neural Filters offer a remarkable solution:

1. **Opening the Image and Accessing Neural Filters:** Open the old photo in Photoshop 2024. Following the steps outlined in Section 5.1 (Accessing the Neural Filters Gallery), navigate to "Filter" > "Neural Filters."
2. **Applying a Style Transfer Effect:** Within the Style Transfer category, explore various artistic styles. For this example, consider a "Vintage Comic" style to add a touch of nostalgia and graphic novel flair to the family portrait. Click on the chosen style to apply the effect to your image.
3. **Refining the Result (Optional):** While the initial style transfer might be impressive, you can further refine the outcome using customization options (refer to Section 5.1 for details). For instance, you might adjust the slider for "Style Strength" to achieve a subtler effect or use masking to selectively apply the style to specific areas of the portrait, such as the clothing.

Case Study 2: Transforming Landscapes with the Landscape Mixer

Imagine a breathtaking mountain landscape photo, but the sky lacks drama or visual interest. The Landscape Mixer filter can elevate your image to new heights:

1. **Open the Image and Access Neural Filters:** Open your landscape photo in Photoshop and navigate to "Filter" > "Neural Filters" as described in Section 5.1.
2. **Utilizing the Landscape Mixer:** Within the Landscape Mixer category, browse through various sky presets featuring vibrant sunsets, dramatic cloud formations, or even mystical auroras. Select a sky that complements the mood you want to create in your final image.
3. **Balancing the Blend:** The Landscape Mixer seamlessly blends the skies, but you might want to fine-tune the effect. Look for adjustment options (sliders or blending modes) that allow you to control the intensity of the blended sky or adjust its color balance to create a more harmonious transition with the foreground elements.

Case Study 3: Color Grading with a Twist Using Color Transfer

Color grading is a fundamental image editing technique for enhancing mood and atmosphere. Neural Filters offer a unique twist on this concept with the Color Transfer filter:

1. **Open Your Images and Prepare the Reference Photo:** Open both your main image (the one you want to color grade) and a reference image with a captivating color palette in separate Photoshop documents. The reference image could be anything from a vibrant sunset landscape to a classic movie poster with a specific color scheme.

2. **Accessing Neural Filters and Choosing Color Transfer:** In your main image document, navigate to "Filter" > "Neural Filters" (as described in Section 5.1). Within the Neural Filters Gallery, select the "Color Transfer" filter.
3. **Selecting the Reference Image:** A window might appear prompting you to select a source image. Choose the reference image you prepared in step 1. This action applies the reference image's color palette to your main image, creating a unique and artistic color grading effect.
4. **Optional Adjustments:** Depending on the filter and your desired outcome, you might have further customization options. These might allow you to control the intensity of the color transfer or use masking to selectively apply the effect to specific areas of your image.

Summary

This chapter invites you to embark on a comprehensive exploration of the dynamic realm of Neural Filters within Photoshop 2024, unveiling an innovative technology that harnesses the power of artificial intelligence (AI) to redefine the landscape of image editing. Immerse yourself in a captivating journey of artistic exploration, and discover how Neural Filters offer you a plethora of creative avenues to transform mundane photos into captivating works of art, akin to the strokes of a master painter's brush.

At its core, this chapter meticulously structures your exploration of Neural Filters, beginning with a foundational understanding of their functionalities. It offers you an insightful glimpse into the underlying principles of AI, particularly the role of deep learning algorithms trained on extensive datasets of images and artistic styles. Through this immersive dive into AI, you gain a nuanced appreciation of how these algorithms discern patterns and relationships within data, enabling you to apply diverse artistic styles to your photos with remarkable precision and accuracy.

Central to the chapter's narrative is the Neural Filters Gallery, a captivating workspace where the magic truly unfolds. With detailed instructions and guidance, you'll navigate through an array of filter categories, each housing a diverse spectrum of effects ranging from Style Transfer to Landscape Mixer and Color Transfer. This structured approach not only empowers you to explore the breadth of creative possibilities but also ensures a seamless integration of these advanced tools within the familiar environment of Photoshop.

Moreover, the chapter meticulously showcases some of the most transformative Neural Filters available in Photoshop 2024, each offering unique and compelling capabilities. From the awe-inspiring potential of Style Transfer to the breathtaking imagery achievable with the Landscape Mixer filter, you're invited to envision the myriad ways in which these tools can elevate your creative endeavors. Whether replicating classic art movements or infusing contemporary trends into your photos, Neural Filters empower you to transcend conventional boundaries and unlock new realms of artistic expression.

Furthermore, the chapter extends beyond theoretical exploration, delving into practical applications through inspiring case studies. By witnessing how professional editors leverage Neural Filters, you gain invaluable insights into the real-world impact and potential of these powerful tools. Through detailed walkthroughs and step-by-step instructions, you're equipped with the knowledge and skills to breathe new life into old photos, enhance landscapes, and experiment with creative color grading techniques.

In essence, this chapter serves as a gateway to the vast landscape of creative image manipulation facilitated by Neural Filters. It not only equips you with the technical know-how to navigate these advanced tools but also inspires you to embrace experimentation and explore the endless possibilities for artistic expression. As you embark on your journey armed with newfound skills and inspiration, you're poised to push the boundaries of image editing in Photoshop 2024, ushering in a new era of creativity and innovation.

Review Questions

1. Explain the core functionality of Neural Filters in Photoshop 2024. How does artificial intelligence (AI) play a role in achieving artistic effects?

2. Describe the workflow for using Neural Filters. This explanation should include how to access the Neural Filters Gallery, navigate filter categories, and utilize filter previews.
3. Beyond the specific case studies explored in this chapter, discuss two additional creative applications for Neural Filters in Photoshop 2024. How might you leverage these filters to achieve your artistic vision?

CHAPTER 6: AI-POWERED CONTENT CREATION AND GENERATION

The digital content landscape is undergoing a seismic shift fueled by the ever-evolving power of artificial intelligence (AI). This chapter embarks on a journey to explore the exciting world of AI-powered content creation and generation. We'll unveil the innovative tools and functionalities shaping the future of how we create content across various digital media platforms.

Imagine effortlessly generating compelling text content, from social media posts to captivating blog articles, with the assistance of AI writing companions. Envision bringing your creative ideas to life by using AI tools that generate stunning images and videos – transforming a simple concept into a visually striking masterpiece. The realm of AI-powered content creation even extends to the world of music, empowering the generation of unique melodies and soundscapes that fuel your creative endeavors.

However, the impact of AI extends far beyond the technological marvel. We'll delve into the deeper implications of AI-generated content within the digital media landscape. Explore how these tools revolutionize workflows, enhance efficiency, and potentially democratize content creation by making it more accessible to a wider audience. We'll also examine the evolving expectations of content consumers in a world saturated with AI-generated content.

The conversation doesn't end there. This chapter would be remiss without acknowledging the ethical considerations surrounding AI-generated content. We'll explore critical questions regarding ownership and attribution – who holds the rights to content created with the assistance of AI? Furthermore, we'll examine the potential for bias within AI algorithms and how to mitigate its influence on the content generation process. Finally, we'll address the question of human creativity in the face of AI's growing capabilities. Will AI become a competitor, or can it foster collaboration and propel human creativity to new heights?

This chapter equips you with a comprehensive understanding of AI-powered content creation. By exploring its functionalities, implications, and ethical considerations, you'll gain valuable insights into the future of content creation in the ever-evolving digital world. So, buckle up and get ready to embark on a journey that explores the boundless potential and thought-provoking questions surrounding AI-powered content creation and generation!

6.1 Exploring AI-driven Content Creation Tools and Capabilities

The world of AI-powered content creation is brimming with innovative tools that are transforming the way we approach content generation across various digital media platforms. This section delves into three key areas where AI is making significant strides: text generation, image and video generation, and even music composition.

6.1.1 Text Generation: Unveiling the Power of AI Writing Assistants

Imagine a world where writer's block becomes a relic of the past. AI writing assistants are revolutionizing the way we generate text content. These intelligent tools leverage AI algorithms to analyze vast amounts of text data and learn writing styles, tones, and grammatical structures. This empowers them to assist you in various content creation tasks, including:

- **Content ideation:** Struggling to brainstorm ideas for your next blog post or social media caption? AI writing assistants can help! These tools can generate creative prompts, suggest relevant topics, and even provide outlines to jumpstart your writing process.
- **Content creation:** AI can assist you in crafting compelling and well-structured content. Some writing assistants offer features like

sentence completion or paragraph generation, helping you streamline the writing process and overcome writer's block.
- **Content editing and proofreading:** Don't underestimate the power of AI for revising your work. Writing assistants can identify grammatical errors, suggest stylistic improvements, and ensure your content adheres to specific tone and clarity requirements.

It's important to remember that AI writing assistants are not designed to replace human creativity entirely. They serve as powerful tools to enhance your workflow, overcome writer's block, and generate ideas to fuel your creative content.

6.1.2 Image and Video Generation: From Concept to Creation with AI

The realm of AI-powered content creation extends far beyond the written word. AI image and video generation tools are transforming the way we bring visual concepts to life. These tools allow you to:

- **Generate images from text descriptions:** Imagine describing your dream vacation destination in a few words and having an AI tool generate a stunning image that captures its essence. This technology allows you to create high-quality visuals even if you lack design expertise.
- **Edit and enhance existing images:** AI can assist you in refining and enhancing your existing photos and graphics. Some tools offer features like automatic background removal, object replacement, or color correction, streamlining your image editing workflow.
- **Create video content:** While still in its early stages, AI-powered video generation is a rapidly developing field. Imagine tools that can generate video snippets or even entire video sequences based on your textual descriptions or storyboards.

The potential applications of AI image and video generation tools are vast, spanning creative endeavors like social media content creation, marketing materials development, and even video editing for various media projects.

6.1.3 Music Composition: AI-powered Melodies and Soundscapes

The world of music creation is not immune to the transformative power of AI. AI-powered music composition tools are emerging that allow you to:

- **Generate musical pieces based on genre or mood:** Imagine selecting a specific genre or mood (e.g., uplifting pop or melancholic piano ballad) and having an AI tool generate a complete musical piece that captures that essence. These tools can be a valuable resource for creating background music or soundtracks for various projects.
- **Collaborate with AI to create unique compositions:** Some AI music tools allow you to provide musical building blocks or melodies and then collaborate with the AI to generate variations, harmonies, or entire sections of a song. This fosters a unique creative partnership between human and machine.

While AI-powered music composition is still evolving, it holds immense potential for musicians, producers, and content creators who require royalty-free background music or original compositions for their projects.

As you explore these AI-driven content creation tools, it's important to remember that they are constantly under development. The capabilities and functionalities will continue to improve, offering even more innovative ways to generate and refine content across various digital media platforms. The next section will delve into the broader implications of AI-generated content within the digital media landscape.

6.2 Understanding the Implications of AI-Generated Content in Digital Media

The emergence of AI-powered content creation tools has far-reaching implications for the digital media landscape. This section explores how AI is revolutionizing workflows, democratizing content creation, and potentially influencing consumer expectations.

6.2.1 Revolutionizing Workflows: Efficiency and Time-Saving Benefits

One of the most significant implications of AI-generated content is its potential to streamline content creation workflows and save valuable time.

- **Content ideation and brainstorming:** AI writing assistants can help overcome writer's block and generate creative ideas, freeing up human creators to focus on refining concepts and adding their unique voice.
- **Content production:** AI tools can automate repetitive tasks like generating social media captions, product descriptions, or basic blog post outlines. This allows creators to focus on more strategic aspects of content development.
- **Content editing and revision:** AI-powered editing tools can identify grammatical errors, suggest stylistic improvements, and ensure consistency of tone and clarity. This streamlines the revision process and saves content creators valuable editing time.

By automating these time-consuming tasks, AI empowers content creators to produce content more efficiently and focus on the aspects that require human creativity and strategic thinking.

6.2.2 Democratizing Content Creation: Accessibility and New Opportunities

The emergence of AI-powered content creation tools has the potential to democratize the content creation landscape. Here's how:

- **Lowering the barrier to entry:** AI tools can equip individuals with limited design or writing experience to create high-quality content. For instance, AI image generation tools can help non-designers create visually appealing graphics for social media posts or marketing materials.
- **Increased accessibility for diverse voices:** AI writing assistants can translate languages or adapt content for different audiences. This allows creators to reach a wider audience and share their unique perspectives.
- **Empowering new creators:** The ease of use and affordability of many AI content creation tools empower individuals to experiment and develop their creative skills, fostering a more diverse and inclusive creator landscape.

However, it's important to remember that AI tools are not a replacement for human creativity and expertise. The most effective content will likely be a blend of AI-generated elements and human ingenuity.

6.2.3 Evolving Consumer Expectations: The Future of Content Consumption

The increasing prevalence of AI-generated content will undoubtedly influence consumer expectations. Here's what to consider:

- **Demand for high-quality and personalized content:** Consumers are likely to expect content that is not only visually appealing and well-written but also tailored to their specific interests and preferences. AI can personalize content recommendations and potentially even contribute to the creation of personalized content experiences.
- **Shifting content consumption habits:** The ease and speed of AI-generated content creation could lead to a faster pace of content production and consumption. Consumers may expect a constant stream of fresh content across various platforms.

Understanding these evolving consumer expectations is crucial for content creators who want to remain relevant and engage their audience in the age of AI-powered content generation.

6.3 Ethical Considerations and Implications of AI-Generated Content Creation

The exciting world of AI-powered content creation is not without its complexities. This section explores some of the key ethical considerations that arise alongside this innovative technology.

6.3.1 Ownership and Attribution: Who Owns AI-Generated Content?

As AI plays an increasingly prominent role in content creation, the question of ownership becomes paramount. Who holds the copyright or intellectual property rights to content generated with the assistance of AI?

- **Ownership by Developers:** In some cases, the developers of the AI tool might retain ownership of the content generated using their platform. This raises questions about how creators can leverage AI-generated content for commercial purposes.
- **Joint Ownership:** A more nuanced approach suggests joint ownership between the human creator who provides prompts and edits, and the AI tool that generates the content. This approach requires clear guidelines and legal frameworks to be established.
- **User Ownership:** Some argue that users who interact with the AI tool and provide creative input should be considered the rightful owners of the generated content.

The legal landscape surrounding AI-generated content ownership is still evolving. It's crucial to stay informed about the latest developments and best practices to ensure proper attribution and ownership rights.

6.3.2 Bias and Fairness: Mitigating Algorithmic Bias in AI Content Creation

AI algorithms are trained on massive datasets of text and code. Unfortunately, these datasets can sometimes reflect and perpetuate societal biases. This raises concerns about the potential for AI-generated content to be biased in terms of race, gender, or other social factors.

- **Identifying and Mitigating Bias:** Developers of AI content creation tools need to be proactive in identifying and mitigating bias within their algorithms. This can involve using diverse training datasets and implementing fairness checks throughout the development process.
- **Transparency and User Awareness:** It's essential for users of AI content creation tools to be aware of the potential for bias and to approach the generated content with a critical eye. Fact-checking and verification remain crucial steps in the content creation process.

By fostering transparency and actively mitigating bias, we can ensure that AI-generated content remains fair and promotes inclusive representation.

6.3.3 Impact on Human Creativity: Collaboration or Competition?

The emergence of AI-powered content creation tools raises questions about the future of human creativity. Will AI become a competitor, rendering human creators obsolete? The answer is likely more nuanced.

- **AI as a Collaboration Tool:** AI can be a powerful tool for augmenting human creativity. Imagine using AI to brainstorm ideas, generate variations on concepts, or streamline repetitive tasks. This frees up human creators to focus on higher-level aspects of content creation, such as developing compelling narratives or adding a unique human touch.
- **The Irreplaceable Human Element:** AI may be able to generate impressive content, but it currently lacks the emotional intelligence,

critical thinking, and cultural understanding that human creators possess. These human qualities will remain essential for creating truly impactful and engaging content.

The future of content creation likely lies in a collaborative approach, where AI and human creators work together to leverage the strengths of each. AI can be a powerful tool for enhancing efficiency and exploration, while human creativity remains the driving force behind truly groundbreaking and impactful content.

Summary

This chapter embarked on an exploratory voyage into the exciting realm of AI-powered content creation. We opened a box of innovative tools and functionalities that are revolutionizing the way we generate content across various digital media platforms. From AI writing assistants that craft compelling text to AI image and video generation tools that bring visual concepts to life, the potential applications seem limitless. Even the world of music is not immune to this transformative power, with AI-powered tools emerging to assist in composing melodies and soundscapes.

However, the conversation extends far beyond the technological marvel. We delved into the deeper implications of AI-generated content within the digital media landscape. AI has the potential to streamline workflows by automating repetitive tasks like content ideation and editing, freeing up valuable time for creators to focus on strategic aspects and refine their creative vision. Furthermore, AI-powered tools have the potential to democratize content creation by lowering the barrier to entry and empowering individuals with limited design or writing experience. This fosters a more diverse and inclusive creator landscape, with a wider range of voices reaching a global audience. As AI content generation becomes more prevalent, consumer expectations will undoubtedly evolve. The future holds the possibility of content that is not only high-quality and visually appealing but also personalized to individual interests and preferences.

Content creators will need to adapt to this shifting landscape to remain relevant and engage their audience in an era saturated with AI-generated content.

The journey doesn't end there. This chapter also acknowledged the ethical considerations surrounding AI-generated content. A critical question that arises is the issue of ownership and attribution. Who holds the copyright or intellectual property rights to content created with the assistance of AI? The legal landscape surrounding this question is still evolving, and creators need to stay informed about best practices to ensure proper attribution. Another critical consideration is the potential for bias within AI algorithms. These algorithms are trained on massive datasets, and if these datasets reflect societal biases, the generated content can perpetuate those same biases. Developers of AI content creation tools need to be proactive in identifying and mitigating bias within their algorithms, while users must remain vigilant and approach AI-generated content with a critical eye.

The final frontier explored the potential impact of AI on human creativity. Will AI become a competitor, rendering human creators obsolete? The answer appears to lie in collaboration. AI can be a powerful tool for augmenting creativity, assisting with brainstorming, generating variations on concepts, and streamlining repetitive tasks. This frees up human creators to focus on the irreplaceable aspects of content creation – developing compelling narratives, infusing content with emotional intelligence and critical thinking, and adding a unique human touch. The future of content creation is likely a harmonious collaboration between human and machine, where AI enhances efficiency and exploration, and human creativity remains the driving force behind groundbreaking and impactful content.

By acknowledging and addressing these complexities, we can ensure that AI-powered content creation becomes a force for good. This technology holds the potential to foster creativity, inclusivity, and innovation within the ever-evolving digital media landscape. As we move forward, it's crucial to embrace the potential of AI content creation tools while remaining mindful of the ethical considerations to shape a future where humans and AI work together to create a more vibrant and diverse digital content ecosystem.

Review Questions

1. The chapter explores various AI-powered content creation tools. Discuss two specific tools or functionalities that pique your creative interest. How might you leverage these tools to enhance your own content creation process?
2. The ethical considerations surrounding AI-generated content are crucial. Explain the concept of bias in AI algorithms and discuss two potential strategies to mitigate bias in AI-powered content creation tools.
3. The future of content creation likely lies in collaboration between humans and AI. In your opinion, how can human creators leverage AI tools to augment their creative process while ensuring their own creative voice remains prominent in the final content?

CHAPTER 7: ADVANCED RETOUCHING TECHNIQUES WITH AI ASSISTANCE

Gone are the days of meticulously applying adjustments pixel by pixel. AI-driven tools are revolutionizing the retouching workflow, empowering you to achieve professional-grade results with remarkable precision and efficiency.

Imagine effortlessly smoothing blemishes, achieving flawless skin tones, or even selectively enhancing specific image elements – all with the assistance of intelligent algorithms. This chapter unveils the exciting possibilities of AI-powered retouching, equipping you with the knowledge and skills to elevate your image editing to a whole new level.

Whether you're a seasoned professional editor or an aspiring creative enthusiast, this chapter serves as your comprehensive guide. We'll embark on a journey that explores the following:

- **Mastering the Art of AI-Driven Retouching:** This section lays the foundation, equipping you to identify areas where AI excels in the retouching process. You'll learn to leverage AI-powered filters and adjustments within your editing software, familiarizing yourself with functionalities like automatic skin retouching, selective adjustments based on object recognition, or advanced frequency separation techniques for superior texture control. Crucially, you'll discover how to refine and customize the results generated by AI tools, ensuring your artistic vision shines through.
- **Deep Dive into AI-powered Skin Retouching:** Skin enhancement takes center stage as we delve deeper into the specific functionalities available. Get ready to explore the magic of AI algorithms that analyze and refine skin textures. Discover how these tools achieve flawless yet natural-looking results through intelligent skin smoothing, blemish removal, and targeted adjustments. We'll

also explore advanced skin tone correction techniques that utilize AI to achieve a more even and harmonious color balance within your images. However, the emphasis remains on preserving authenticity – you'll learn how AI tools can be used to enhance skin texture subtly, maintaining natural details like freckles or wrinkles for a realistic and captivating final image.

- **Navigating the Ethical Landscape of AI Retouching:** The power of AI comes with a responsibility to use it ethically. This section addresses crucial considerations that ensure your retouching practices promote positive values. We'll discuss the importance of maintaining realistic beauty standards and avoiding the distortion of natural features. Transparency with clients regarding the use of AI tools will be emphasized, along with strategies for open communication that establishes realistic expectations and ensures client satisfaction. Finally, we'll delve into the art of subtle yet impactful retouching. The most effective retouching often goes unnoticed, achieving a natural and believable final image that enhances the subject's beauty without appearing overly manipulated.

By the conclusion of this chapter, you'll be well-equipped to leverage AI-powered retouching tools effectively within your image editing workflow. We'll provide detailed instructions and practical guidelines for each technique, empowering you to achieve professional-grade results while maintaining artistic control and ethical considerations.

7.1 Mastering Advanced Retouching Techniques with AI-driven Tools in Photoshop 2024

The world of image retouching has transformed with the introduction of AI-powered tools in Photoshop 2024. These tools streamline the process, allowing you to achieve professional-grade results with precision and efficiency. This section equips you to leverage AI effectively within your retouching workflow in Photoshop 2024.

1. Identifying Tasks Well-Suited for AI Assistance:

While AI excels in specific areas, it's important to strategically utilize it to optimize your workflow. Here are some prime candidates for AI assistance in Photoshop 2024:

- **Skin Retouching:**
    - **Skin Smoothing:** Locate the "Skin Smoothing" filter by navigating to **Filter > Noise > Skin Smoothing**. This filter analyzes and refines skin texture, offering adjustments for smoothing strength, blemish reduction, and detail preservation using convenient sliders.
    - **Reduce Noise:** For general noise reduction, access the "Reduce Noise" filter at **Filter > Noise > Reduce Noise**. Target unwanted grain or noise, particularly in low-light images.
- **Noise Reduction with Subject Selection:** For more precise noise reduction, explore the "Select Subject" tool and the "Reduce Noise" filter in tandem. Here's how:
    - **Select Subject:** Go to the **Select** menu and choose **Subject**. This tool uses AI to identify the foreground subject and create a selection around it.
    - **Targeted Noise Reduction:** With your subject selected, navigate to **Filter > Noise > Reduce Noise**. This allows you to target noise reduction specifically in the background area while leaving your subject untouched.
- **Selective Adjustments:** Leverage the power of "Selective Adjustments" to target specific areas within your image. Here's how to find it:
    - **Selective Adjustments Panel:** Go to **Layer > New Adjustment Layer > Selective Color**. This opens the

"Selective Adjustments" panel, allowing you to choose a specific color range (e.g., blues for sky replacement) and adjust its properties like brightness, saturation, or hue. This way, you can selectively enhance the sky without affecting the rest of the image.

2. Leveraging AI-powered Filters and Adjustments in Photoshop 2024:

Photoshop 2024 integrates a plethora of AI-powered filters and adjustments. Let's explore some noteworthy features:

- **Automatic Skin Retouching Filters:** Access a treasure trove of filters by navigating to **Filter > Filter Gallery**. The "Portrait" category offers AI-powered options like "Skin Smoothing" or "Reduce Noise" (discussed previously). These filters provide a one-click solution for basic skin retouching, with sliders for customization like smoothing intensity or noise reduction levels.
- **AI-powered Frequency Separation with Skin Retouching:** While not directly an AI filter, Photoshop 2024's "Frequency Separation" technique can be combined with AI tools for advanced texture control. Here's a step-by-step approach:
    1. **Duplicate Layer:** Begin by duplicating your image layer. You can achieve this by right-clicking on the layer in the Layers panel and selecting "Duplicate Layer" or pressing Ctrl/Cmd + J.
    2. **High Pass Filter:** Navigate to **Filter > Other > High Pass**. This filter creates a mask that separates texture from color information. Adjust the slider to define the cutoff frequency between these elements. A higher value targets broader textures like wrinkles, while a lower value focuses on finer details.
    3. **Splitting Color and Texture:** This step creates two separate layers. Click "OK" on the "High Pass" filter window. You'll now see two layers in your Layers panel – one containing the

color information and the other containing the texture details.
4. **Applying AI Skin Retouching:** With the color layer selected, utilize AI skin retouching filters like "Skin Smoothing" (discussed earlier) to refine skin texture while preserving details on the texture layer.
5. **Reuniting Layers:** Once satisfied with the color adjustments, adjust the blending mode of the texture layer (located in the Layers panel next to the layer opacity) to control how the texture overlays the color information. For subtle texture overlay, try "Soft Light" blending mode. Experiment with different blending modes to achieve the desired effect.

- **Object-Aware Adjustments with Select Subject:** Photoshop 2024's "Select Subject" tool again plays a crucial role in object-aware adjustments. Here's the workflow:
  1. **Subject Selection:** Use the "Select Subject" tool (**Select > Subject**) to isolate your subject. This creates a selection around the foreground object.
  2. **Targeted Adjustments:** With your subject selected, explore various tools for selective adjustments:
     - **Selective Adjustments Panel:** As discussed earlier, navigate to **Layer > New Adjustment Layer > Selective Color** to target specific color ranges. This allows for adjustments like brightening the sky or enhancing the color of a specific object without affecting the selected subject.
     - **Brush Tool with Adjustment Layers:** For more precise control, use the "Brush Tool" (located in the Toolbar) in conjunction with adjustment layers. Here's how:

1. **Create an Adjustment Layer:** Click the "Create new adjustment layer" icon at the bottom of the Layers panel and choose the desired adjustment type (e.g., Levels for brightness/contrast adjustments, Curves for advanced tonal adjustments).
2. **Refine Selection (Optional):** If needed, further refine your selection using tools like "Refine Edge" (located under the "Select" menu when you have a selection active) to ensure clean edges around your subject before applying adjustments.
3. **Brush Tool Adjustments:** Select the "Brush Tool" and adjust its brush settings (size, hardness) in the Options bar at the top. Choose black paint for darkening or white paint for lightening on the adjustment layer mask (a small, black and white mask thumbnail next to the adjustment layer in the Layers panel). Painting with white reveals the adjustment effect in the desired areas, while painting with black hides it. This allows you to selectively brighten specific areas (e.g., highlights on hair) or darken specific areas (e.g., background shadows) without affecting the selected subject.

3. Refining and Customizing AI-generated Results in Photoshop 2024:

Even with the power of AI, human expertise remains paramount. Here's how to refine and customize AI-generated results in Photoshop 2024:

- **Masking Techniques:** Mastering masks allows for precise control over adjustments. When using AI skin retouching filters, create a mask on the "Skin Smoothing" adjustment layer by clicking the mask thumbnail next to the layer in the Layers panel. Here's how to utilize the mask for selective adjustments:

- o **Hiding Smoothing Effect:** Paint black on the mask with the "Brush Tool" (as discussed earlier) to hide the smoothing effect in areas where you want to preserve texture details (e.g., eyebrows, eyelashes). Black on the mask conceals the adjustment layer's effect in those areas.
- o **Revealing Smoothing Effect:** Conversely, paint white on the mask with the "Brush Tool" to reveal the smoothing effect in desired areas. White on the mask allows the adjustment layer's effect to show through.

- **Selective Adjustments:** Even with AI-powered object recognition, further refinement might be necessary. Use adjustment layers and the "Brush Tool" as described earlier to selectively adjust specific areas. For instance, you might use a Curves adjustment layer to brighten a specific area of the sky that the "Selective Color" adjustments missed.
- **Maintaining Artistic Control:** Remember, AI is a tool, not a replacement for your artistic vision. Use these functionalities as a starting point, and customize the results to achieve the specific look and feel you desire for your image. Don't be afraid to experiment with different tools and blending modes to achieve your creative goals.

7.2 Exploring AI-powered Skin Retouching and Texture Enhancements in Photoshop 2024

The realm of skin retouching has been revolutionized by AI. This section dives deeper into the specific functionalities available within Photoshop 2024, empowering you to achieve flawless yet natural-looking results. Here, we'll explore tools and techniques to target blemishes, adjust skin tones, and preserve natural textures, all with the assistance of intelligent algorithms.

1. AI-powered Skin Smoothing and Blemish Removal:

- **Skin Smoothing Filter:** Locate the "Skin Smoothing" filter by navigating to **Filter > Noise > Skin Smoothing**. This filter analyzes skin texture and offers adjustments for smoothing strength, blemish reduction, and detail preservation using convenient sliders.
    - **Smoothing:** This slider controls the overall smoothness of the skin. Adjust it cautiously to avoid an overly plastic appearance. Aim for subtle adjustments that enhance skin texture without going overboard.
    - **Reduce Noise:** Use this slider to target unwanted grain or texture, particularly helpful in low-light portraits where camera noise might be more prominent.
    - **Detail:** This slider preserves a certain level of skin texture for a more natural look. Adjust it to prevent the skin from looking overly blurred. Find a balance between smoothing imperfections and maintaining a natural level of detail.
- **Spot Healing Brush with AI:**

- The "Spot Healing Brush" tool (located in the Toolbar under the "Healing Brush" tool) is a powerful tool for blemish removal, and Photoshop 2024 integrates AI to make it even more effective. Here's how to use it:
    - **Sample Source:** Hold down the **Alt/Option** key (depending on your operating system) and click on a clean area of skin next to the blemish. This defines the source area used for the healing process. The AI algorithm will analyze this area and use its texture to seamlessly replace the blemish.
    - **Brush Size:** Adjust the brush size (in the Options bar at the top of the workspace) to match the size of the blemish you want to remove. A brush size slightly larger than the blemish will ensure complete coverage.
    - **Brush over Blemish:** Click and drag the brush over the blemish. AI analyzes the surrounding area and seamlessly replaces the blemish with texture from the chosen source area.

2. Advanced Skin Tone Correction and Color Balancing:

- **Selective Color Adjustments:** As discussed earlier, the "Selective Color" adjustment layer allows you to target specific color ranges within the image. Access it by navigating to **Layer > New Adjustment Layer > Selective Color**. In the context of skin retouching, you can use this tool for:
    - **Reducing Redness:** Click on the "Reds" channel in the adjustment layer window. Decreasing the saturation of the "Reds" channel helps reduce skin redness, particularly around the nose or cheeks. Use subtle adjustments to avoid a washed-out appearance.

- **Balancing Skin Tones:** Click on the "Neutrals" or "Skin Tones" channels (if available) and adjust their saturation and hue for subtle color correction and evening out skin tones. Again, prioritize subtle adjustments for a natural look.
- **Color Balance Adjustment Layer:** For more precise color adjustments, explore the "Color Balance" adjustment layer. Find it by going to **Layer > New Adjustment Layer > Color Balance**. This layer offers independent adjustments for highlights, midtones, and shadows, allowing you to fine-tune skin tones across different tonal ranges within the image:
  - **Highlights:** Use the sliders in the "Highlights" section to adjust the color balance specifically in the brighter areas of the skin (e.g., forehead, cheekbones).
  - **Midtones:** The sliders in the "Midtones" section target the most prominent skin tones within the image. Use them for overall color adjustments.
  - **Shadows:** The sliders in the "Shadows" section affect the darker areas of the skin (e.g., under the chin, around the eyes). Adjust them subtly to address color casts or imbalances in these areas.

3. Preserving Natural Skin Texture with AI:

While achieving a flawless appearance is desirable, it's crucial to maintain a natural look. Here's how to utilize AI tools while preserving texture:

- **Frequency Separation with Skin Smoothing:** The technique explored earlier (duplicate layer, High Pass filter, separate color and texture layers) allows for selective smoothing. Here's a quick refresher:
  1. **Duplicate Layer:** Begin by duplicating your image layer. Right-click on the layer in the Layers panel and select "Duplicate Layer" or press Ctrl/Cmd + J.

- **High Pass Filter (Continued):** Go to **Filter > Other > High Pass**. This filter creates a mask that separates texture from color information. Adjust the slider to define the cutoff frequency between these elements. A higher value targets broader textures like wrinkles, while a lower value focuses on finer details. 3. **Splitting Color and Texture:** Click "OK" on the "High Pass" filter window. You'll now see two layers in your Layers panel – one containing the color information (bottom layer) and the other containing the texture details (top layer). 4. **Applying AI Skin Retouching:** With the color layer selected (bottom layer), utilize AI skin retouching filters like "Skin Smoothing" (discussed earlier) to refine skin texture. Adjust the sliders (Smoothing, Reduce Noise, Detail) to achieve the desired level of smoothing while preserving some texture details in the layer. 5. **Reuniting Layers:** Once satisfied with the color adjustments on the bottom layer, adjust the blending mode of the texture layer (top layer) located in the Layers panel next to the layer opacity. The blending mode controls how the texture overlays the color information. For subtle texture overlay that maintains natural details, try "Soft Light" blending mode. Experiment with different blending modes to achieve the effect you desire.
- **Brush Tool with Overlay Blending Mode:** For targeted smoothing in specific areas while preserving texture, use the "Brush Tool" with an adjustment layer in "Overlay" blending mode. Here's the workflow:
    1. **Create Levels Adjustment Layer:** Click the "Create new adjustment layer" icon at the bottom of the Layers panel and choose "Levels." This adjustment layer allows for adjustments to brightness, contrast, and shadows/highlights specifically in the areas you target with the brush.
    2. **Brush Tool Adjustments:** Select the "Brush Tool" from the Toolbar. Adjust the brush size (in the Options bar at the top) to match the area you want to target for smoothing. Choose

black paint on the mask of the Levels adjustment layer (the small, black and white mask thumbnail next to the Levels adjustment layer in the Layers panel). Painting with black on the mask darkens those specific areas in the image. This can be useful for subtle smoothing of blemishes or uneven skin tone. The "Overlay" blending mode preserves some texture details while achieving a smoothing effect. Use light brush strokes and adjust the opacity of the brush (also in the Options bar) for more precise control.

By following these steps and using these functionalities strategically, you can leverage AI-powered retouching tools in Photoshop 2024 to achieve natural-looking skin enhancements while maintaining a healthy balance between smoothing imperfections and preserving essential texture details. The next section will address crucial considerations for ethical and responsible use of AI retouching tools.

7.3 Ethical and Responsible Use of AI Retouching Tools

The power of AI-powered retouching tools in Photoshop 2024 comes with a responsibility to use them ethically and responsibly. This section equips you with best practices to ensure your edits are truthful, respectful, and promote realistic beauty standards.

1. Maintaining Authenticity and Transparency:

- **Selective Adjustments over Global Filters:** While AI skin smoothing filters offer a one-click solution, they can lead to unnatural-looking results if applied globally. Focus on selective adjustments using techniques like:
    - **Spot Healing Brush:** As discussed earlier (**Toolbar > Spot Healing Brush**), target blemishes and imperfections for a more natural approach.

- - **Brush Tool with Adjustment Layers:** Utilize the "Brush Tool" (**Toolbar**) with adjustment layers (e.g., Levels) to target specific areas for adjustments like smoothing or color correction. This allows for more precise control over the retouching process. Refer to section 7.2.3 for a detailed breakdown of this technique.
- **Before-and-After Comparisons:** Maintain transparency throughout your workflow. Create duplicate copies of your image at various stages of retouching to compare and ensure you're not going overboard with AI smoothing.

2. Respecting Individuality and Diversity:

- **Preserving Skin Texture:** Don't erase all skin texture in pursuit of a flawless look. Use AI skin smoothing filters (section 7.2.1) cautiously and prioritize maintaining natural details like freckles or subtle wrinkles. Techniques like frequency separation (section 7.2.3) allow you to refine skin texture on the color layer while preserving details on the texture layer.
- **Embracing Diverse Beauty Standards:** AI retouching shouldn't be used to conform to narrow beauty ideals. Avoid drastically altering facial features or body shapes to fit unrealistic stereotypes. Celebrate diversity and represent a wider range of beauty in your edits.

3. Avoiding Misrepresentation and False Advertising:

- **Disclosure of AI Retouching:** If you're using AI retouching tools for professional purposes (e.g., advertising, commercial photography), disclose this information. Transparency builds trust with your audience and avoids accusations of misrepresentation.
- **Focus on Enhancing Natural Beauty:** The goal of retouching should be to enhance natural beauty, not create a completely fabricated image. Use AI tools to subtly remove blemishes, even

skin tone, or brighten the eyes. Avoid dramatic alterations that misrepresent the subject's appearance.

These guidelines help you harness the potential of AI retouching tools in Photoshop 2024 while upholding ethical principles and promoting a more realistic and inclusive vision of beauty in your image editing endeavors.

Summary

This chapter explored the exciting world of AI-powered retouching in Photoshop 2024. You learned how to leverage AI tools to achieve professional-grade results with precision and efficiency. Here's a quick recap:

- **Identify tasks well-suited for AI:** Focus on repetitive tasks like skin smoothing, noise reduction, and selective adjustments using the "Skin Smoothing" filter, "Reduce Noise" filter, and "Selective Color" adjustment layer.
- **Utilize AI-powered filters and adjustments:** Explore the "Skin Smoothing" filter for one-click adjustments, "Frequency Separation" for advanced texture control, and "Select Subject" for object-aware adjustments.
- **Refine and customize AI-generated results:** Master masking techniques with the "Brush Tool" to selectively adjust specific areas and preserve natural details. Utilize adjustment layers like "Levels" and "Curves" for further refinement.
- **Explore AI-powered skin retouching:** Utilize the "Spot Healing Brush" with AI for blemish removal. Target skin tone corrections with "Selective Color" and "Color Balance" adjustment layers.
- **Maintain natural skin texture:** Apply AI skin smoothing cautiously and explore techniques like frequency separation to preserve details. Use the "Brush Tool" with "Overlay" blending mode for targeted smoothing while retaining texture.

- **Practice ethical and responsible retouching:** Maintain authenticity with selective adjustments and before-and-after comparisons. Respect individuality by preserving skin texture and embracing diverse beauty standards. Disclose AI retouching for professional uses and focus on enhancing natural features.

By following these tips and delving deeper into the techniques explored in this chapter, you can transform your retouching workflow in Photoshop 2024 and achieve stunning results that are both beautiful and realistic.

Review Questions

1. When retouching skin texture with AI tools in Photoshop 2024, what are two techniques you can use to preserve natural details while achieving a smoothed appearance
2. Imagine you're retouching a portrait for commercial purposes. How can you ethically leverage AI tools in Photoshop 2024 to enhance the image while maintaining transparency and avoiding misrepresentation?
3. Beyond the tools covered in this chapter, what other factors do you think are important for achieving successful and natural-looking retouching using Photoshop 2024.

CHAPTER 8: STREAMLINING WORKFLOWS WITH AUTOMATION AND AI SCRIPTS

Ready to take your editing efficiency to the next level? This chapter dives into the exciting world of automation and AI scripts in Photoshop 2024. We'll explore how to harness the power of pre-programmed actions and artificial intelligence to streamline repetitive tasks, save you time, and potentially open doors to creative possibilities you never imagined. Buckle up and get ready to transform the way you work in Photoshop!

8.1 Harnessing the Power of Automation with Photoshop Scripts and Actions

Ever feel bogged down by repetitive tasks in Photoshop 2024? Imagine if you could automate those time-consuming edits, freeing yourself to focus on the creative aspects of image manipulation. This section unlocks the potential of built-in automation features – **scripts and actions**.

These powerhouses go beyond simple keyboard shortcuts. Scripts and actions allow you to record entire sequences of steps you take within Photoshop, essentially creating a digital recipe for editing tasks. Once recorded, you can replay these actions on other images with a single click, saving you countless hours and ensuring consistent results.

Here, we'll embark on a journey to understand the core functionalities of scripts and actions. We'll explore the specific tasks they can automate and the incredible efficiency gains they offer. You'll learn the art of recording your actions, capturing that magic sequence you use for a specific edit. We'll also delve into editing and modifying these recordings, allowing you to fine-tune them for optimal performance. Finally, get ready to unleash the power of batch processing with actions. This incredible feature allows you to automate edits for a whole folder of images at once, transforming your workflow from tedious to triumphant.

By mastering these functionalities, you'll be well on your way to streamlining your editing process. Scripts and actions will become your secret weapons, helping you conquer repetitive tasks and unleash your creative potential within Photoshop 2024.

8.1.1 Understanding Scripts and Actions: Building Blocks of Automation

The ever-evolving landscape of Photoshop offers powerful tools to streamline your workflow and free you to focus on creative expression. This section dives into the foundational concepts of **scripts and actions**, built-in automation features within Photoshop 2024. Understanding their capabilities will empower you to transform repetitive tasks into effortless processes.

Scripts vs. Actions: What's the Difference?

While both scripts and actions automate tasks, there are key distinctions to consider:

- **Scripts:** These are like mini-programs written in a specific scripting language (e.g., JavaScript, ExtendScript) that offer a high degree of flexibility and customization. Scripts can access a wider range of Photoshop functionalities and perform complex calculations, making them ideal for intricate tasks or integrating with external tools.
- **Actions:** These are recorded sequences of steps you take within Photoshop. Imagine creating a macro for a specific editing process – actions capture those steps, allowing you to replay them on other images with a single click. Actions are user-friendly and ideal for automating common, well-defined tasks like resizing images, applying filters, or creating watermarks.

The Benefits of Automation:

Here's why incorporating scripts and actions into your workflow is a game-changer:

- **Increased Efficiency:** Imagine the time saved by automating repetitive tasks. Scripts and actions free you to focus on the creative aspects of image editing, boosting your overall productivity.
- **Consistency:** Actions ensure consistent results across multiple images. This is particularly valuable for tasks like batch processing photos with the same edits.
- **Reduced Error:** By automating repetitive tasks, you minimize the risk of human error that can occur during manual editing.

Ready to explore the exciting world of automation? The next sections will equip you with the skills to record your own actions, edit and modify them for optimal performance, and unlock the power of batch processing.

8.1.2 Recording Your First Action: Capturing the Magic

Repetitive tasks can feel like a creativity drain. Wouldn't it be liberating to automate those edits and dedicate your energy to the artistic aspects of image manipulation? This section equips you with the power to record your own actions in Photoshop 2024, essentially creating a digital recipe for your most frequently used edits.

Locating the Actions Panel:

The first step on your automation journey is accessing the Actions panel. Here's how to find it:

1. **Navigate to the Window Menu:** Look for the "Window" menu at the top of your workspace in Photoshop 2024.

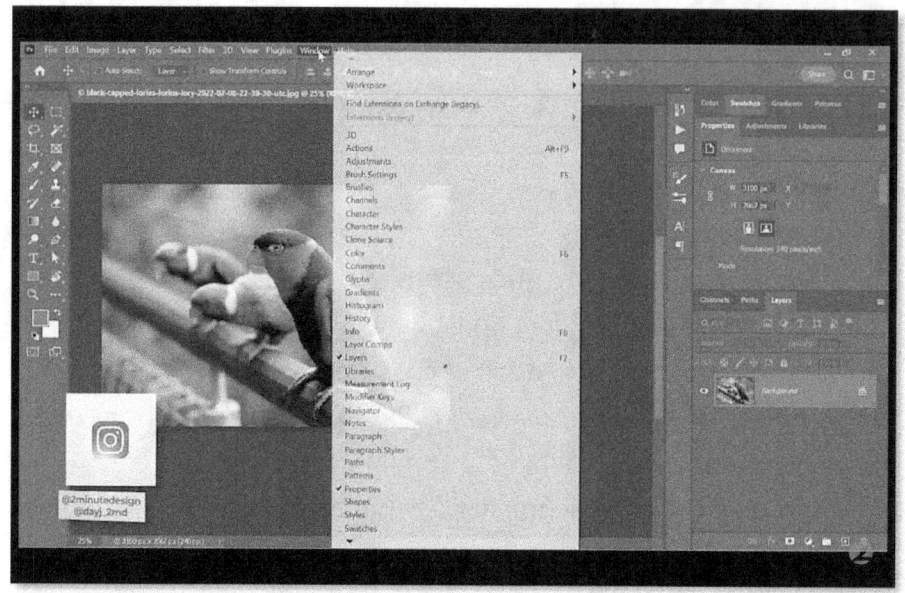

2. **Select Actions:** Click on the "Actions" option within the "Window" menu. This will open the Actions panel, which will typically dock on the right side of your workspace.

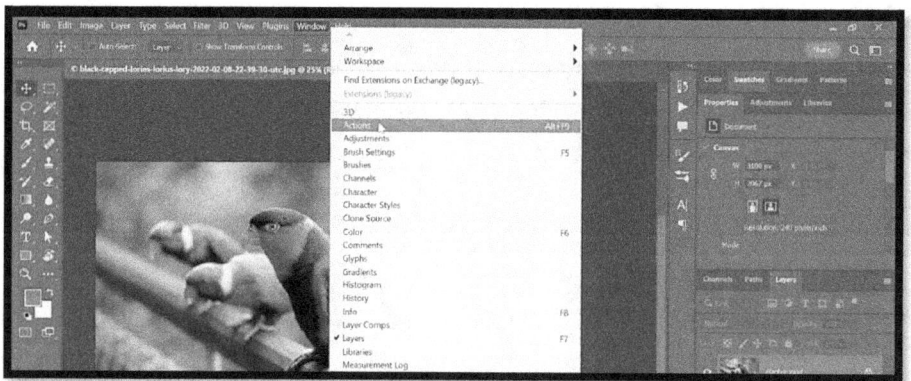

Recording Your Action:

With the Actions panel open, you're ready to capture your editing magic:

1. **Click the "Create New Set" Icon:** In the Actions panel, locate the small folder icon with a plus sign (+) in the top right corner. This signifies creating a new set to organize your actions. Clicking this icon will prompt you to name your new set (e.g., "Basic Edits").
2. **Click the "Create New Action" Icon:** Next to the "Create New Set" icon, you'll find another icon resembling a play button with a recording symbol. Clicking this icon initiates the action recording process. A new action will appear within your chosen set, ready to capture your steps.

3. **Perform Your Desired Edits:** Now comes the fun part! Hit record and begin editing your image as you normally would. Every step you take, from selecting tools to adjusting sliders, will be recorded within the action. For best practice, consider performing clear and well-defined edits that you'd like to automate.

4. **Click the "Stop Recording" Button:** Once you've completed your desired edits, locate the square red button within the Actions panel (usually next to the recording icon). Clicking this button stops the recording process, finalizing your newly created action.

Congratulations! You've successfully recorded your first action in Photoshop 2024. The next section will guide you through refining and customizing these recorded actions for optimal performance.

8.1.3 Editing and Modifying Recorded Actions: Fine-tuning Your Automation

You've embarked on the path to automation by recording your first action in Photoshop 2024. Now let's explore how to refine and customize these recordings to ensure they function flawlessly and meet your specific needs.

Accessing Your Recorded Action:

Within the Actions panel, navigate to the set you created (e.g., "Basic Edits") and locate your newly recorded action (e.g., "Resize and Sharpen"). Clicking on the action name highlights it, allowing you to edit its properties.

Modifying Action Steps:

- **Double-click the Action Name:** This opens the "Actions" window, displaying a list of all the steps you recorded within the action. Each step details the specific tool used, adjustments made, and menu selections.
- **Editing Individual Steps:** Here, you can edit specific steps within your action. For instance, you might want to adjust a slider value used in a filter or modify the selection size for a cropping tool. Simply click on the desired step and make the necessary changes in the "Options" panel on the right side of the window.
- **Reordering Steps:** The order of steps within an action is crucial. Use the up and down arrow buttons located next to each step in the "Actions" window to rearrange them if needed. This ensures the action playback follows the intended sequence.

Adding Pauses and Dialog Boxes:

- **Pausing the Action:** In some cases, you might want the action to pause during playback, prompting you for user input. For example, you could insert a pause before a "Save As" step, allowing you to choose a specific filename and location each time the action runs. Click the "Insert Pause" icon (resembles a pause symbol) at the bottom of the "Actions" window to add a pause point.
- **Capturing Dialog Boxes:** If your action involves using a tool with a dialog box (e.g., "Curves" adjustment), you can choose to capture the specific settings used. During recording, ensure the "Capture Tool Specific Options" checkbox within the Actions panel options (usually a gear icon) is selected. This will record the values used in the dialog box, ensuring they're replicated during playback.

Testing and Refining:

- **Playtesting the Action:** With your edits complete, it's time to test your action. Click the "Play" button (triangle symbol) next to the action name in the Actions panel. The action will playback on your current image, mimicking the steps you recorded. Observe the process closely to ensure each step executes as intended.
- **Refine and Repeat:** If you encounter any issues during playback, simply return to the "Actions" window and make the necessary adjustments to the steps. Test and refine your action until it functions flawlessly.

These editing and modification techniques helps you to transform your recorded actions into powerful tools within your Photoshop 2024 workflow. The next section delves into the incredible efficiency gains offered by batch processing with actions.

8.1.4 Batch Processing with Actions: Automating Edits for Multiple Images

Imagine editing a folder full of images and applying the same set of adjustments to each one. The thought can be daunting. This is where **batch processing with actions** comes to the rescue! By leveraging the power of actions you've recorded, you can automate edits for a multitude of images at once, saving you significant time and effort.

The Batch Processing Powerhouse:

- **Navigate to the Automate Menu:** Within the top menu bar of Photoshop 2024, locate the "Automate" menu.
- **Select Batch:** Click on the "Batch" option within the "Automate" menu. This opens the "Batch" window, your gateway to automated editing bliss.

Setting Up Batch Processing:

1. **Choose Your Action:** In the "Batch" window, the first crucial step is selecting the action you want to apply to your images. Use the dropdown menu under "Action" to choose the action you've created (e.g., "Resize and Sharpen").
2. **Define Your Source Folder:** Click the "Browse" button next to "Source" and specify the folder containing the images you want to edit in batch. This tells Photoshop where to locate the images for processing.
3. **Choose Your Destination Folder (Optional):** While optional, specifying a destination folder (using the "Browse" button next to "Destination") allows you to save the edited images in a separate location from the originals.
4. **Refine Your Options (Optional):** The "Batch" window offers additional options for further customization. For instance, you can choose to name the edited files using a specific naming pattern or skip processing any images that encounter errors.

Hitting the Green Button:

Once you've configured the settings in the "Batch" window, you're ready to unleash the power of automation. Click the "OK" button, and Photoshop 2024 will spring into action. It will silently process each image in your source folder, applying the selected action and saving them according to your defined destination (if chosen).

Sit back, relax, and witness the magic of automation! Batch processing with actions transforms repetitive tasks into a breeze, freeing you to focus on other creative endeavors within Photoshop.

Bonus Tip: For even greater efficiency, consider combining actions. Create separate actions for individual editing steps (e.g., resize, sharpen, watermark) and then record a master action that plays them back sequentially. This allows you to build complex editing workflows that can be automated with a single click during batch processing.

By mastering these functionalities, you've unlocked a powerful arsenal of automation tools within Photoshop 2024. With recorded actions and batch processing, you can streamline your workflow, conquer repetitive tasks, and dedicate more time to the artistic aspects of image editing.

8.2 Creating Custom AI-driven Scripts for Task Automation and Optimization

In this section, we're diving into the world of scripting. Specifically, we're going to explore how you can create your own custom scripts that use artificial intelligence (AI) to automate tasks and make your Photoshop workflow smoother.

Ever wished you could automate repetitive tasks and focus more on your creative process? That's exactly what custom scripts can help you with. We'll walk you through the basics of scripting in Photoshop, show you how to integrate AI functionalities, and even provide examples of how to build your own custom scripts.

Whether you're new to scripting or looking to level up your Photoshop skills, this section is here to help you make the most out of your creative journey.

8.2.1 Introduction to Photoshop Scripting Languages

Understanding Scripting Languages:

Before scripting magic can unfold, it's important to grasp the language Photoshop 2024 understands. The primary scripting languages used are:

- **JavaScript:** A versatile and widely popular scripting language, well-suited for automating tasks within Photoshop. If you're new to scripting, JavaScript offers a gentle learning curve.
- **ExtendScript:** Developed specifically for Photoshop scripting, ExtendScript provides a powerful and efficient way to interact with the application's functionalities.

Scripting Fundamentals: Building Blocks for Automation

Let's break down the essential concepts you'll encounter in scripting:

- **Variables:** These act like containers that store data used within your script. For instance, you can create a variable to store an image path or a specific adjustment value.
- **Conditional Statements:** These statements allow your script to make decisions based on certain conditions. Imagine a script that checks the image size and resizes only if it exceeds a specific dimension.
- **Loops:** These repetitive code blocks allow your script to execute a sequence of steps multiple times. This is particularly useful for automating tasks on a series of images.

By mastering these fundamentals, you'll lay the foundation for crafting powerful and efficient scripts in Photoshop 2024.

8.2.2 Creating Your First Script Using Actions: A Basic Tutorial for Automation in Photoshop

Introduction:

In Photoshop, scripts are powerful tools that can automate repetitive tasks, saving you time and effort. In this tutorial, we'll walk through the process of creating your first script to automate a simple task. By the end, you'll have a basic understanding of how scripts work and how they can enhance your workflow in Photoshop.

Step 1: Understanding Scripts

Before we begin creating our script, let's recap what scripts are and understand how they work in Photoshop. A script is a set of instructions that tells Photoshop to perform certain actions automatically. These actions can range from simple tasks like resizing images to more complex operations like batch processing.

Step 2: Choosing a Task

For our first script, let's choose a simple task to automate. A common task is resizing images to a specific width and height. This is something you might do often when preparing images for a website or social media.

Step 3: Recording the Script

To create our script, we'll use the Script Editor in Photoshop. Go to File > Scripts > Script Editor to open the Script Editor window. Next, go to the Actions panel (Window > Actions) and click on the "Create new action" button. Give your action a name, like "Resize Images," and click Record to start recording your actions.

Step 4: Performing the Task

Now, perform the task you want to automate. In this case, open an image in Photoshop and resize it to your desired width and height using the Image Size option (Image > Image Size). Once you're done resizing the image, stop recording your action by clicking on the stop button in the Actions panel.

Step 5: Saving the Script

With the action recorded, we can now save it as a script. Go back to the Script Editor window and click on the "Save as" button. Choose a location to save your script and give it a name, like "ResizeImages.jsx". Make sure to select the ".jsx" file format, which is the file format for Photoshop scripts.\

Step 6: Running the Script

To test your script, close the image you used to record the action and open a new image. Now, go to File > Scripts > Browse and navigate to the location where you saved your script. Select the script file and click Open. Photoshop will automatically resize the image according to the actions recorded in the script.

Congratulations! You've created your first script in Photoshop. Scripts are powerful tools that can automate a wide range of tasks, helping you work more efficiently. Experiment with different tasks and explore the capabilities of scripts to further enhance your workflow in Photoshop.

Learning Resources:

The internet provides a wealth of resources for learning JavaScript and scripting for Photoshop. The world of scripting awaits you with just one internet search.

Remember: This is just a basic example using recorded actions to create scripts. As you delve deeper into scripting, you'll learn how to leverage variables, conditional statements, and loops to create more complex and powerful scripts that automate tasks and integrate with AI functionalities within Photoshop 2024.

8.2.3 Integrating third-party AI tools and APIs for enhanced functionality

This section will sink a layer deeper into scripting, utilizing some advanced scripting concepts that enable the integration of third-party APIs (Application Programming Interface) to foster more robust editing in Photoshop 2024. This section requires that you already understand some basic scripting concepts like variables, conditionals, promises, asynchronous operations, loops, and libraries like axious for sending HTTP requests to third-party APIs.

Introduction to AI Integration in Scripts: Exploring the Role of Third Party AI tools in Task Automation

Artificial Intelligence (AI) integration in scripts opens up a world of possibilities for task automation and optimization within Photoshop. AI-powered scripts can analyze, process, and enhance images with remarkable precision and efficiency. By leveraging AI, scripts can perform tasks that traditionally required manual intervention, such as image enhancement, style transfer, object recognition, and much more.

The integration of AI in scripts revolutionizes the way we approach image editing tasks. Instead of relying solely on predefined rules and algorithms, AI-powered scripts can adapt and learn from vast datasets to produce intelligent and context-aware results. This level of automation not only saves time but also ensures consistent and high-quality outcomes across a variety of editing tasks.

Step-by-step Script Construction: Constructing a Custom Script that Utilizes AI Functionalities

Now, let's dive into the process of constructing a custom script that harnesses the power of AI functionalities. We'll break down the steps involved in creating a script that calls an external AI library to enhance image editing tasks.

1. Define the Objective: Start by clearly defining the objective of your script. What specific task or tasks do you want the script to automate or optimize using AI?

2. Research AI Libraries: Explore available AI libraries that offer functionalities relevant to your objective. Look for libraries that specialize in image processing, enhancement, or style transfer.

3. Choose a Programming Language: Select a programming language that is compatible with both Photoshop scripting and the chosen AI library. JavaScript is commonly used for scripting in Photoshop.

4. Set Up Development Environment: Set up your development environment with the necessary tools and dependencies. This may include installing the chosen AI library and any additional software required for script development.

5. Write Script Code: Begin writing the script code, incorporating calls to the AI library functions. This code will define the logic and functionality of your script, specifying how it interacts with Photoshop and utilizes AI for image enhancement tasks.

6. Test and Debug: Test your script thoroughly to ensure it functions as intended. Debug any errors or issues that arise during testing, refining the script code as needed for optimal performance.

Practical Use Case: Creating a Script that Calls an External AI Library to Enhance Image Editing Tasks

Let's dive into a real-life use case: creating a script that utilizes an external AI library to automatically remove background from images in Photoshop. We'll go through each step, including finding a suitable AI library, writing the script in JavaScript, and testing it in Photoshop.

1. Objective Definition: Our objective is to create a script that automates the process of removing backgrounds from images in Photoshop using AI-powered algorithms.

2. AI Library Research: After researching available AI libraries, we find an AI image processing library called "RemoveBG" that specializes in background removal tasks. We can find this library at remove.bg.

3. Programming Language Selection: We choose JavaScript as the programming language for scripting in Photoshop, as it is compatible with both Photoshop scripting and the RemoveBG API.

4. Development Environment Setup:

   a. Install Node.js: We install Node.js, a JavaScript runtime, on our computer by following the instructions on the Node.js official website. Node.js will allow us to make HTTP requests to the RemoveBG API from our script.

   b. Install Axios: We use the Axios library, a popular HTTP client for Node.js, to make HTTP requests to the RemoveBG API. We install Axios using the following command in the terminal:

  npm install axios

5. Script Code Writing: We write the script code in a text editor. Below is the code for our script:

```javascript
// Importing required libraries

import axios from 'axios';

const axios = require('axios');

const fs = require('fs');
```

```javascript
// Function to remove background using RemoveBG API
async function removeBackground(imagePath) {
    try {
        // Make POST request to RemoveBG API
        const response = await axios.post( [[ RemoveBG endpoint ]],
            fs.createReadStream(imagePath),
            {
                headers: {
                    'X-Api-Key': 'YOUR_API_KEY' // Replace 'YOUR_API_KEY' with your actual RemoveBG API key
                },
                responseType: 'stream'
            }
        );

        // Save the processed image
        response.data.pipe(fs.createWriteStream('output.png'));

        return 'Background removed successfully!';
```

```
    } catch (error) {

        return 'Error removing background: ' + error.message;

    }

}
```

```
// Call the removeBackground function with the path to the image

removeBackground('input.jpg')

    .then(message => console.log(message))

    .catch(error => console.error(error));
```

Note: Replace ``YOUR_API_KEY`` with your actual RemoveBG API key and [[RemoveBG endpoint]] with the actual RemoveBG endpoint.

6. Testing and Debugging: We save the script as `removeBackground.js` and run it using Node.js in the terminal:

```
node removeBackground.js
```

The script will process the image `input.jpg`, remove the background using the RemoveBG API, and save the result as `output.png`.

7. Testing in Photoshop: Finally, we open Photoshop and import the original image along with the processed image (`input.jpg` and `output.png`). We verify that the background has been successfully removed from the processed image.

By following these steps, we have created a custom script that integrates an external AI library to remove backgrounds from images in Photoshop automatically. This practical example demonstrates the power of AI integration in scripts for streamlining image editing tasks.

Summary

This chapter explored the exciting realm of automation and AI-powered scripts within Photoshop 2024. You learned valuable strategies to streamline your workflow and conquer repetitive tasks.

- **Harnessing Built-in Automation:** We delved into **actions**, powerful tools that record your editing steps, allowing you to replay them on other images with a single click. You discovered how to record, edit, and modify actions for optimal performance. Furthermore, **batch processing with actions** was introduced, a method to automate edits for a folder full of images at once.
- **Building Custom Scripts:** The chapter ventured into the world of **custom scripting**, empowering you to create your own mini-programs that automate tasks beyond the capabilities of actions. We explored popular scripting languages (JavaScript, ExtendScript) and fundamental scripting concepts like variables, conditional statements, and loops. A basic JavaScript script example was provided to get you started on your scripting journey.
- **AI Integration Potential:** The chapter highlighted the possibilities of **AI-driven scripts**. These scripts can leverage external AI libraries to perform tasks like facial recognition or object detection, allowing you to automate complex editing processes within Photoshop.

By mastering the techniques covered in this chapter, you can transform your workflow in Photoshop 2024. Automation and scripting will become your allies, freeing you from repetitive tasks and allowing you to focus on the creative aspects of image editing.

Review Questions

1. You're tasked with resizing and sharpening a batch of 50 product images for your online store. How would you leverage automation features in Photoshop 2024 to accomplish this task efficiently? Explain the process in detail
2. Imagine you want to create a script that automatically reduces noise in night photographs while preserving details. Briefly explain the key functionalities this script would need and discuss the potential challenges you might encounter during the scripting process.
3. Beyond the functionalities covered in this chapter, what other factors do you think are important for creating effective and user-friendly custom scripts in Photoshop 2024.

CHAPTER 9: INTEGRATING 3D AND AUGMENTED REALITY WITH PHOTOSHOP

The domain of image manipulation is poised for a significant transformation. Envision the integration of lifelike 3D models into your artwork or the development of engaging Augmented Reality (AR) encounters that merge the digital and tangible realms. This is no longer a concept confined to futuristic narratives—it's the thrilling reality within the Photoshop 2024 ecosystem!

This section reveals the capabilities of 3D and AR integration. We're about to dive into an exploration of the fundamental principles of 3D modeling and AR, examining how these technologies can be effectively utilized within Photoshop to craft compelling and interactive visual narratives.

Unraveling the Mysteries of 3D and AR: We'll dissect the essentials of incorporating 3D models within Photoshop, equipping you with the abilities to smoothly import, manipulate, and render them within your compositions. Additionally, you'll gain a deeper understanding of the principles behind AR and how Photoshop facilitates the creation of these immersive experiences.

Leveraging AI for Interactive AR: Prepare to unlock the untapped potential of AI-driven object recognition. Discover how Photoshop harnesses AI to automatically identify objects in your images, setting the stage for interactive AR experiences. Imagine spectators using their smartphones to activate 3D models or animations based on the objects they observe in your image—the possibilities are virtually limitless!

Transforming Design and Narrative: This section delves into the transformative impact of 3D and AR on interactive design and storytelling. Learn how to craft captivating design presentations that showcase your work in a new light. We'll also explore innovative techniques for integrating these elements into your stories, enhancing audience engagement.

By diving into this section, you'll acquire the knowledge and abilities to effectively utilize 3D and AR within Photoshop 2024. Get set to push the boundaries of creativity and create visuals that will astound and leave a lasting impact. Let's initiate this thrilling exploration!

9.1 Exploring the Convergence of 3D Modelling and Augmented Reality in Photoshop

The world of image editing is undergoing a seismic shift. Photoshop 2024 embraces this evolution by seamlessly integrating **3D modelling** and **Augmented Reality (AR)**
functionalities. This section lays the foundation for your exploration by demystifying these powerful tools and their incredible potential within your creative workflow.

9.1.1 Understanding 3D Integration

Traditionally, Photoshop excelled in manipulating 2D imagery.
Now, with 3D integration, you can incorporate **3D models** – digital representations of 3D
objects – into your compositions. This opens doors to a whole new realm of
creative possibilities:

- **Product visualization:** Imagine showcasing a new furniture design by placing a detailed 3D model into a room setting. Clients can virtually "walk around" the furniture, gaining a more realistic sense of scale and detail.
- **Enhanced packaging design:** Create eye-catching packaging mockups by integrating 3D models of your product onto a realistic background.
- **Concept art and illustration:** Breathe life into your illustrations by incorporating 3D models as a base for characters, objects, or environments.

9.1.2 Demystifying Augmented Reality

Imagine a world where digital elements seamlessly blend with the real world. This is the essence of **Augmented Reality (AR)**. AR overlays virtual objects onto the real world viewed through a smartphone or tablet camera. Photoshop 2024 empowers you to create these AR experiences, allowing viewers to interact with your creations in a whole new way.

Consider these exciting possibilities:

- **Interactive marketing campaigns:** Imagine a brochure where viewers can point their smartphone camera at a specific product image and see a 3D model come alive on their screen, showcasing its features in an interactive way.
- **Educational AR experiences:** Create AR overlays for museum exhibits that allow visitors to view additional information or 3D models of historical artifacts by pointing their devices at specific displays.
- **Enhanced product experiences:** Develop AR apps that allow customers to virtually place furniture pieces within their homes before making a purchase decision.

The potential applications of AR are vast and constantly evolving.

The next section will explore the synergy between 3D and AR, highlighting the incredible possibilities that arise when you combine these powerful technologies within Photoshop 2024.

9.1.3 The Power of Combining 3D and AR: Blurring the Lines Between Reality and Imagination

The magic truly unfolds when you combine the power of 3D modelling and Augmented Reality (AR) within Photoshop 2024. Imagine placing a **realistic 3D model** – a car, a piece of furniture, even a fantastical creature – into a real-world scene using AR. The possibilities for creative expression are truly boundless! Here are some captivating applications:

Interactive design presentations: Revolutionize the way you showcase your design work. Create AR experiences where clients can view 3D models of your designs superimposed onto real-world environments. Imagine presenting a new building design by allowing clients to virtually "walk around" it within the context of the planned construction site using AR.

Immersive storytelling: Elevate your narratives to a whole new level by incorporating 3D and AR elements. Imagine a children's book where illustrations come alive in AR, allowing young readers to interact with 3D characters or objects by pointing their smartphones or tablets at specific pages.

- **Bringing imagination to life:**

The combination of 3D and AR opens doors for boundless creativity. Imagine creating an AR experience where viewers can point their devices at a blank canvas and see a 3D model of a fantastical creature they've designed come to life before their eyes.

By harnessing the synergy between 3D and AR in Photoshop 2024, you'll be able to create immersive and interactive experiences that blur the lines between reality

and imagination. This powerful combination will leave a lasting impression on

your audience and push the boundaries of visual storytelling.

9.2 Creating Immersive AR Experiences with AI-powered Object Recognition

Unleash the Power of AI for Interactive AR

Imagine creating AR experiences where viewers can point their smartphones or tablets at your images and trigger interactive elements based on the objects they see. This is no longer science fiction – it's within reach with Photoshop 2024's **AI-powered object recognition** and AR integration features. Let's dive into how to leverage this exciting functionality.

9.2.1 Leveraging AI for Object Recognition in Your Images

The magic behind interactive AR experiences with AI object recognition lies in **training Photoshop to identify specific objects** within your images. Here's a breakdown of the process:

1. **Prepare Your Image:** Open your image in Photoshop 2024 and ensure it's clear and well-lit for optimal AI recognition.
2. **Access the Object Selection Tool:** Navigate to the "Select" menu in the top toolbar and choose "Object Selection Tool" (alternatively, press "Shift + W").
3. **Train the AI:** With the Object Selection Tool active, click and drag a rectangular marquee around the object you want the AI to recognize. A pop-up window will appear. Here's the key step:
    - **Name the Object:** In the pop-up window, assign a clear and specific name to the object you've selected. For instance, if

it's a shoe in your image, name it "Shoe." This name will become the trigger for your AR interaction.
4. **Train More Objects (Optional):** If your image contains multiple objects you want the AI to recognize, repeat step 3 for each one, assigning unique names. The more objects you train the AI on, the richer your AR experience can become.

By following these steps, you've essentially "taught" Photoshop to identify the specific objects within your image. This paves the way for incorporating interactive AR elements based on these recognized objects.

9.2.2 Building Interactive AR Experiences with Recognized Objects

Now that the AI can recognize your objects, let's explore how to create interactive AR experiences within Photoshop 2024:

1. **Access the AR Authoring Tool (Beta):** While still under development, Photoshop 2024 offers a built-in AR Authoring Tool (Beta). Navigate to the "Window" menu and select "AR (Beta)". **Note:** As it's a beta feature, functionalities may be subject to change in future updates.
2. **Link Recognized Objects to AR Elements:** Within the AR Authoring Tool window, you'll see a list of the objects you trained the AI to recognize in your image (e.g., "Shoe"). Here, you can link each object to a specific AR element:
    - **Text Overlay:** Choose to display text information about the object when it's viewed in AR. Imagine an AR experience where viewers see the word "Running Shoe" displayed above the recognized shoe in your image when they point their device at it.
    - **3D Model Overlay:** Link a 3D model to the recognized object. This allows viewers to see a 3D version of the object come alive in AR. Imagine showcasing a 3D model of the

shoe from different angles when viewers interact with your AR experience.
- **Animation or Video Overlay:** For a more dynamic experience, you can choose to display an animation or video clip that plays when the object is recognized in AR.

By linking these interactive elements to the recognized objects, you've transformed your static image into an engaging AR experience!

Important Note: While Photoshop 2024 provides AR authoring functionalities, exporting your AR experience likely requires additional software or collaboration with AR development platforms. This section focused on creating the interactive elements within Photoshop, but keep in mind there might be additional steps for final AR deployment.

By following these steps and exploring the functionalities within the AR Authoring Tool (Beta), you can unlock the potential of AI object recognition to create interactive and captivating AR experiences that will grab your audience's attention. The next section will delve into how 3D and AR can be leveraged for interactive design and storytelling applications.

9.2.3 Real-world Applications: Bringing AR Experiences to Life

The possibilities for AR experiences powered by AI object recognition are vast and constantly evolving. Here's a glimpse into how various industries are leveraging this technology to create engaging and informative applications:

- **E-commerce:** Imagine product packaging that comes alive with AR. Customers can point their smartphones at the packaging and see additional product information, detailed 3D models, or even interactive tutorials on how to use the product – all triggered by the AI recognizing specific objects on the packaging. This can enhance the customer experience and provide a more immersive way to learn about products.

Creating an AR Experience for E-commerce Packaging:

1. **Design your product packaging:** Create clear and high-quality visuals for your packaging that showcase the product effectively.
2. **Identify key objects for recognition:** Decide which elements on the packaging you want the AI to recognize for AR interactions. This could be the product logo, specific features of the product itself, or even informational icons.
3. **Train the AI in Photoshop:** Following the steps in section 9.2.1, open your packaging design in Photoshop and use the Object Selection Tool to train the AI on each object you want to trigger AR interactions. Assign clear and descriptive names to each object during training (e.g., "Logo," "Main Feature," "Instruction Icon").
4. **Link AR elements in the AR Authoring Tool:** Access the AR Authoring Tool (Beta) as explained in section 9.2.2. Here, link each recognized object to the desired AR element. You can choose to display text information about the product when viewers hover over the logo with their device, showcase a 3D model of the product when they point at the main feature image, or even trigger a short video demonstrating how to use the product when they interact with the instruction icon.

- **Education:** Museums and historical sites can utilize AR to create interactive exhibits. Imagine visitors pointing their devices at artifacts and seeing additional information displayed, 3D models come alive to showcase the object in its historical context, or even hear narrated audio descriptions triggered by the AI recognizing specific objects within the exhibit.

Creating an AR Experience for Museum Exhibits:

1. **Prepare high-resolution images of exhibits:** Ensure you have clear and well-lit photographs of the artifacts or historical objects you want to include in the AR experience.

2. **Identify key objects for recognition:** Decide which specific objects within the exhibit you want the AI to recognize for AR interactions. This could be the entire artifact itself, specific details or features, or informational plaques displayed near the object.
3. **Train the AI in Photoshop:** Following the steps in section 9.2.1, use the Object Selection Tool to train the AI on each object you want to trigger AR elements within your exhibit images. Assign clear and informative names during training (e.g., "Ancient Vase," "Hieroglyphic Inscription," "Information Plaque").
4. **Link AR elements in the AR Authoring Tool:** Within the AR Authoring Tool, link the recognized objects to relevant AR elements. You can display detailed text information about the artifact, showcase a 3D model that allows viewers to rotate and examine the object in detail, or even trigger narrated audio descriptions that play when visitors point their devices at specific features.

- **Marketing and Advertising:** Create interactive AR campaigns that grab attention and leave a lasting impression. Imagine magazine advertisements where viewers can point their smartphones at specific products and see them come alive in 3D, or billboards that display interactive elements triggered by AI object recognition.

Creating an AR Experience for Magazine Advertisements:

1. **Design your print advertisement:** Create an eye-catching advertisement layout that showcases the product you want to promote.
2. **Identify key objects for recognition:** Decide which elements within the advertisement you want the AI to recognize for AR interactions. This could be the product itself, the brand logo, or even specific call-to-action elements.
3. **Train the AI in Photoshop:** Following the steps in section 9.2.1, use the Object Selection Tool to train the AI on each object you want to trigger AR elements within your advertisement design. Assign clear

and descriptive names during training (e.g., "Product Image," "Brand Logo," "Call to Action Button").
4. **Link AR elements in the AR Authoring Tool:** Within the AR Authoring Tool, link the recognized objects to engaging AR elements. You can display additional product information when viewers hover over the product image, showcase a 3D model that allows for a 360-degree view, or even link the call-to-action button to a website or interactive promotion that opens when viewers tap on it with their device.

9.3 Leveraging 3D and AR for Interactive Design and Storytelling

The power of 3D and Augmented Reality (AR) extends far beyond product visualization and marketing campaigns. This section explores how you can harness these technologies within Photoshop 2024 to create interactive design presentations and captivating storytelling experiences.

9.3.1 Enhanced Design Presentations: From Static to Immersive

Gone are the days of flat, static design presentations. Imagine showcasing your work in a whole new dimension with the help of 3D and AR:

- **Product Design:** Instead of presenting static product renderings, incorporate 3D models into your presentation. Allow clients to virtually "walk around" your design in a 3D environment, giving them a more comprehensive understanding of scale, detail, and functionality.
- **Architectural Design:** Revolutionize how you present architectural proposals. Create AR experiences that allow clients to virtually "walk through" a proposed building design within the context of the planned construction site. Imagine them using their smartphones or tablets to view the building from different angles and explore its interior spaces.

- **Interactive Prototypes:** Develop interactive prototypes using 3D and AR. Present website or app design concepts where clients can interact with elements and experience the user interface in a more immersive way.

Here's how to get started with incorporating 3D and AR into your design presentations:

1. **Utilize 3D design software:** There are various 3D design software options available. Learn the basics of 3D modeling to create your own models or acquire pre-made models from online libraries.
2. **Import 3D models into Photoshop:** Once you have your 3D models, import them into Photoshop 2024 for further manipulation and integration into your presentation slides.
3. **Explore AR presentation options:** While Photoshop's AR Authoring Tool (Beta) is still under development, explore third-party AR presentation platforms that allow you to integrate 3D models and create interactive AR experiences for your audience.

Incorporating 3D and AR into your design presentations transforms them from static deliveries to engaging and interactive experiences that will leave a lasting impression on your clients.

9.3.2 Captivating Storytelling Techniques: Beyond the Page

The boundaries of storytelling are dissolving with the power of 3D and AR. Imagine these possibilities:

- **Interactive Children's Books:** Bring children's books to life with AR. Incorporate 3D models or animations that appear when readers point their devices at specific illustrations, creating a more immersive and engaging reading experience.
- **Interactive Educational Materials:** Revolutionize how students learn. Develop AR-enhanced educational materials where students can interact with 3D models of historical artifacts, explore virtual

environments related to scientific concepts, or even manipulate 3D objects to understand complex processes.
- **Immersive Product Narratives:** Showcase your products within a captivating story. Imagine creating AR experiences where viewers can virtually "place" your product within a specific setting and see how it interacts with the environment, all while following a narrative that highlights its functionalities and benefits.

Here are some steps to consider when incorporating 3D and AR into your storytelling:

1. **Develop a clear narrative:** Before integrating 3D and AR elements, ensure you have a strong core story to tell. These technologies will enhance your narrative, not replace it.
2. **Identify opportunities for AR interaction:** Pinpoint specific moments within your story where AR can elevate the experience. Consider where 3D models, animations, or text overlays triggered by AR would best complement your narrative flow.
3. **Utilize user-friendly AR creation tools:** Explore AR creation tools designed for non-programmers. These can help you integrate 3D models and create basic AR interactions without complex coding requirements.

By weaving 3D and AR elements into your storytelling, you'll create **dynamic and immersive experiences** that will capture your audience's imagination and leave a lasting impact.

9.3.3 The Future of Creative Expression: Boundless Potential

The convergence of 3D, AR, and Photoshop 2024 opens doors to a future of boundless creative expression. Imagine these possibilities:

- **Interactive Art Installations:** Develop AR art installations that allow viewers to interact with your artwork in a whole new way.

Imagine sculptures that come alive with AR animations or paintings that transform when viewed through a smartphone camera.

- **Virtual Reality (VR) Storytelling:** The future holds exciting possibilities for combining 3D models and AR experiences within VR environments, creating truly immersive and interactive stories.

- **Unforeseen Innovations:** As these technologies continue to evolve, we can expect even more groundbreaking applications emerge in various fields. Imagine architects collaborating with engineers in VR to design and test complex structures virtually, or fashion designers creating interactive clothing prototypes that customers can virtually try on before purchasing. The possibilities are truly endless!

Here are some additional tips to stay ahead of the curve and harness the potential of 3D and AR for creative expression:

- **Embrace Continuous Learning:** The landscape of 3D design and AR development is constantly evolving. Dedicate time to learning new skills, exploring emerging software, and staying updated on the latest trends in these fields.
- **Experiment and Explore:** Don't be afraid to experiment and push the boundaries of what's possible. Combine 3D and AR with other creative mediums like photography, video, or animation to see what unique experiences you can create.
- **Collaborate with Others:** The power of creative expression often stems from collaboration. Seek out partnerships with 3D designers, AR developers, or storytellers from other disciplines to bring your ideas to life in innovative ways.

By embracing these technologies and fostering a spirit of exploration, you can become a pioneer in shaping the **future of creative expression** with Photoshop 2024 as your launchpad.

Summary

We explored the exciting integration of 3D modeling and Augmented Reality (AR) within Photoshop 2024. You gained the knowledge to import, manipulate, and render 3D models, transforming static images into interactive experiences. We delved into the power of AI object recognition, allowing viewers to trigger 3D elements based on objects identified within your images.

The chapter further explored how to leverage 3D and AR for captivating design presentations and storytelling techniques. We discussed creating presentations that showcase your work in a whole new dimension, alongside crafting interactive narratives that leave a lasting impact.

By incorporating the practical steps and functionalities within Photoshop 2024, you've unlocked a new frontier for creative expression. This chapter empowered you to harness the power of 3D and AR to create groundbreaking visuals and interactive experiences. You are now prepared to push the boundaries of creativity and embark on a journey into the future of visual design and storytelling!

Review Questions

1. How can AI-powered object recognition be leveraged within Photoshop 2024 to create interactive AR experiences? Explain the process of training the AI to recognize specific objects within an image.
2. Describe two ways that 3D modeling and Augmented Reality (AR) can be used to enhance design presentations within Photoshop 2024.
3. Beyond the information covered in this chapter, discuss a creative concept of your own that utilizes 3D or AR technology for storytelling purposes. How would you use Photoshop 2024 to contribute to this concept?

CHAPTER 10: DESIGNING FOR WEB AND MOBILE WITH AI INTEGRATION

The landscape of web and mobile design is undergoing a revolution. Artificial intelligence (AI) is rapidly transforming the way we create digital experiences, offering exciting possibilities for streamlining workflows, optimizing designs, and crafting user-centric interfaces. This chapter unveils the power of AI integration within Photoshop 2024, equipping you with the knowledge and tools to design for the future.

Get ready to explore:

- **AI-powered design automation:** Discover how AI can assist with repetitive tasks, freeing you to focus on the creative aspects of design.
- **Intelligent responsive layouts:** Learn how to leverage AI for responsive web design, ensuring your creations adapt seamlessly across various devices.
- **Data-driven user experience (UX) design:** Delve into how AI-powered analytics can provide valuable user insights, guiding you towards creating user-centered interfaces.
- **The future of AI in design:** Explore emerging AI technologies and discuss ethical considerations for responsible implementation within your design workflow.

By embracing AI as a powerful collaborator, you'll be able to design for web and mobile platforms with unmatched efficiency and user-centric focus. This chapter will equip you with the knowledge and tools to craft cutting-edge digital experiences that will not only look stunning but also provide an intuitive and engaging experience for your users. Let's embark on this exciting journey into the future of web and mobile design with AI by our side!

10.1 Streamlining Responsive Design with AI: Unleashing the Power of AI-powered Layout Suggestions

The ever-growing landscape of devices, from desktops and laptops to tablets and smartphones with various screen sizes and resolutions, presents a constant challenge for web and mobile designers. Ensuring your meticulously crafted design translates flawlessly across all these devices requires a responsive design approach. Traditionally, this involves manually creating and adjusting layouts for each screen size, a time-consuming and often tedious process. However, **AI-powered layout suggestions** within Photoshop 2024 are revolutionizing responsive design, offering an **intelligent and efficient** way to achieve optimal user experience across all platforms.

10.1.1 Unveiling the Magic of AI-powered Layout Suggestions

Imagine this: you've poured your creative energy into designing a stunning website layout on your desktop. But the thought of meticulously recreating and adjusting that layout for various tablet and smartphone screens fills you with dread. AI-powered layout suggestions come to the rescue! Leveraging the power of artificial intelligence, Photoshop 2024 analyzes your design, understanding the relationships and hierarchy between different elements within your layout. This could include text boxes, images, buttons, navigation menus, and any other visual components that make up your web or mobile app interface. By analyzing these elements and their interactions, the AI can generate intelligent layout suggestions optimized for various screen sizes.

Here's a breakdown of how AI-powered layout suggestions work in Photoshop 2024:

1. **Preparing Your Design:** Open your web or mobile app design in Photoshop 2024. Ensure your layout is well-defined and all

elements are placed intentionally within the canvas. The more organized and clear your initial design, the better the AI can understand its structure and generate effective suggestions.

2. **Accessing the AI Layout Suggestion Feature:** While this feature might still be under development or hidden within an experimental tools menu (depending on your specific version of Photoshop 2024), keep an eye out for functionalities like "**Generate Responsive Layouts**" or "**AI-powered Design Variations**." These options might be located within the "Design" or "File" menus, or even as a dedicated button within the workspace.

3. **Specifying Screen Sizes:** Once you've accessed the AI layout suggestion feature, you'll likely be prompted to specify the target screen sizes you want to generate layouts for. This could include common tablet resolutions (e.g., iPad Portrait, iPad Landscape) or popular smartphone sizes (e.g., iPhone X, various Android phone models). The more specific you are about your target devices, the more tailored the AI-generated layouts will be.

4. **AI Analyzes and Generates Suggestions:** Here's where the magic happens! The AI engine within Photoshop 2024 goes to work, analyzing your design, its elements, and their relationships. Based on this analysis, it generates layout variations optimized for the screen sizes you specified. These variations might involve rearranging elements, resizing components, or even hiding/showing specific elements based on the limitations or functionalities of smaller screens.

5. **Reviewing and Implementing AI Suggestions:** Photoshop 2024 will likely present you with a set of AI-generated layout suggestions for each targeted screen size. These suggestions will be displayed alongside your original design, allowing you to easily compare and evaluate their effectiveness. You can choose to implement an entire AI-generated layout with a single click, or use it as a starting point for further adjustments based on your design preferences. The AI

suggestions are meant to be a foundation upon which you can build, not a rigid replacement for your creative vision.

Here are some additional tips for utilizing AI-powered layout suggestions effectively:

- **Don't be afraid to experiment:** Try generating layouts for multiple screen sizes and explore the different variations the AI suggests. This can spark new ideas and help you visualize how your design will adapt across various devices.
- **Consider the context:** While AI can offer intelligent suggestions, it's important **to** review them with the user experience (UX) in mind. Think about how users will interact with your design on different devices and make adjustments if necessary to ensure optimal usability.
- **Maintain design consistency:** While layouts might adapt for different screen sizes, strive to maintain a cohesive visual identity throughout your design. Use consistent colors, fonts, and branding elements to create a seamless user experience across all platforms.

experiences that flawlessly adapt to the ever-evolving landscape of devices. The next section explores another powerful approach to responsive design – adaptive design techniques – and how AI can further enhance this workflow.

10.1.2 Mastering Adaptive Design Techniques with AI Integration

Responsive design ensures your layouts adapt to various screen sizes, but adaptive design takes it a step further. It involves creating multiple, pre-defined layouts specifically tailored for different device categories (e.g., desktops, tablets, smartphones) while maintaining a consistent design language. This approach offers more control over the user experience on each device type.

While traditional adaptive design requires manually creating and iterating on these layouts, AI in Photoshop 2024 can augment your workflow in several ways:

- **Smart Asset Creation:** Imagine creating core design elements (like buttons, navigation menus, or header sections) as **Smart Objects** within Photoshop. These intelligent objects can be easily resized and adapted to different layouts while maintaining their original properties (e.g., text styles, layer effects). This streamlines the process of creating variations for different screen sizes within your adaptive design approach.
- **AI-powered Content Optimization:** Content like images and text can be optimized for various screen sizes using AI functionalities. Photoshop 2024 might offer features like content-aware scaling or automatic text reflowing based on AI analysis of the content and the target device layout. This ensures your content remains visually appealing and readable across different screen sizes.
- **Context-aware Design Variations:** With adaptive design, you might create specific layouts for portrait and landscape orientations on mobile devices. AI can analyze your design and suggest alternative layouts optimized for each orientation. This can involve automatically hiding or rearranging elements based on the screen's physical position.

By combining AI-powered suggestions with your creative control in adaptive design, you can achieve a highly optimized and user-centric experience across various devices. The possibilities are constantly evolving, and future versions of Photoshop might offer even more sophisticated AI functionalities specifically tailored for responsive and adaptive design workflows.

Remember, AI is a powerful tool to augment your design process, not replace your creativity. Use it to your advantage to streamline tasks, explore possibilities, and ultimately craft exceptional user experiences for web and mobile platforms. The next section delves into the power of AI for user-centered design, where user research and data analysis come together to inform your design decisions

10.2 User-Centered Design with AI: Unveiling User Behavior Through AI Analytics

User-centered design (UCD) is the cornerstone of creating successful web and mobile experiences. It emphasizes understanding your users' needs, behaviors, and pain points to craft interfaces that are not only visually appealing but also intuitive and functional. Traditionally, user research involves techniques like surveys, user testing, and A/B testing, which can be time-consuming and resource-intensive. However, AI integration within Photoshop 2024 empowers you to **leverage AI analytics** and gain valuable user insights to inform your design decisions in a more **efficient and data-driven** way.

10.2.1 Integrating User Research with AI Analytics

Imagine being able to analyze user behavior patterns and understand how users interact with your designs directly within Photoshop 2024. This is the potential of AI-powered user analytics.

- **Understanding AI-powered user behavior analysis:** Photoshop 2024 might integrate with web analytics tools or have built-in functionalities that can analyze user behavior data from live websites or mobile applications. This data could include information like click-through rates on buttons, time spent on specific sections of a page, or user scroll patterns. The AI engine can then analyze these behavioral patterns and identify areas where users might be facing difficulties or confusion within your design.
- **Utilizing AI insights to inform user-centered design decisions:** By understanding how users interact with your design, you can make informed decisions to improve the overall user experience.

For instance, AI analytics might reveal that users struggle to find a specific call-to-action button on your website. Based on this insight, you can reposition or redesign the button to make it more prominent and user-friendly. Similarly, AI analysis might show that users tend to scroll past a crucial section of your mobile app. This could prompt you to rethink the layout or incorporate visual cues to draw attention to that particular section.

AI-powered user analytics empowers you to move beyond guesswork and base your design decisions on real user behavior. This ensures you're creating interfaces that are not only aesthetically pleasing but also intuitive and meet the needs of your users. The next section will delve into how AI can further streamline your design workflow within Photoshop 2024.

10.3 Optimizing Design Workflows with AI

The repetitive tasks that often slow down the design process can be significantly alleviated with the help of AI. Photoshop 2024 offers functionalities that leverage AI to automate these tasks, freeing you to focus on the more creative aspects of design.

10.3.1 Exploring AI Tools for Design Automation

Imagine a scenario where AI can handle tedious tasks like background removal, object selection, or image resizing, allowing you to dedicate your time to crafting the core visual elements of your design. Let's delve into some potential AI-powered design automation tools within Photoshop 2024:

- **AI-powered Background Removal:** Struggling with complex selections to isolate objects from their backgrounds? AI can come to the rescue! Photoshop 2024 might offer features that utilize AI to analyze an image and automatically remove the background with impressive accuracy. This can save you hours of meticulous selection work and allow you to seamlessly integrate your objects into new design layouts.

- **Smart Object Manipulation with AI:** Smart Objects are a powerful feature in Photoshop that allows you to resize, distort, and manipulate objects without losing image quality. Imagine combining this functionality with AI. Photoshop 2024 might offer tools that leverage AI to intelligently resize or adjust Smart Objects while maintaining their visual integrity. This can be particularly helpful when creating responsive web designs that need to adapt to various screen sizes.

- **AI-assisted Content Generation:** Content creation can be a time-consuming aspect of design. Photoshop 2024 might introduce AI functionalities that can generate placeholder content like stock images or lorem ipsum text. While this AI-generated content might not be the final solution, it can serve as a starting point for your design, allowing you to focus on the overall layout and user experience before investing time in creating final content.

By identifying repetitive tasks within your design workflow and exploring the AI automation tools available in Photoshop 2024, you can significantly streamline your design process. This frees you to dedicate more time and energy to the creative aspects of design, like crafting unique visual elements, user interfaces, and overall brand experiences. The next section will explore the exciting possibilities that lie ahead in the future of AI-powered web and mobile design.

10.4 The Future of AI-powered Web and Mobile Design

The integration of AI within design tools like Photoshop 2024 is still evolving, and the future holds exciting possibilities for web and mobile design. This section explores some emerging AI technologies that could revolutionize the design landscape, along with the importance of responsible AI implementation.

10.4.1 Emerging AI Technologies for Design

Here's a glimpse into some potential future functionalities powered by AI that could transform web and mobile design:

- **AI-driven Design Inspiration:** Imagine an AI assistant that can analyze your design style and generate creative suggestions for layouts, color palettes, or even typographic choices. This could spark new ideas and help you overcome creative roadblocks.
- **Personalized User Interface (UI) Design:** AI could analyze user data and preferences to create personalized UI experiences. For instance, an e-commerce platform might use AI to tailor product recommendations and layouts based on a user's browsing history.
- **Voice-controlled Design Tools:** The ability to interact with design tools using voice commands could significantly improve workflow efficiency. Imagine sketching out your design ideas verbally and having Photoshop 2024 translate them into visual elements.
- **AI-powered Accessibility Checks:** Ensuring your designs are accessible to everyone is crucial. AI could analyze your web or mobile app and identify potential accessibility issues, allowing you to create inclusive user experiences from the start.

These are just a few examples, and the possibilities are constantly expanding. As AI continues to evolve, we can expect even more innovative functionalities to emerge within design tools, further blurring the lines between human creativity and machine intelligence.

10.4.2 Ethical Considerations and Responsible Use of AI

While AI offers a wealth of potential benefits for design, it's crucial to consider the ethical implications of its implementation. Here are some key points to remember:

- **Identifying Potential Biases:** AI algorithms are trained on data sets, and these data sets can sometimes contain biases. It's

important to be aware of these potential biases and how they might influence the design suggestions generated by AI tools.
- **Ensuring Responsible Use of AI:** As designers, we have a responsibility to use AI tools ethically. Don't blindly accept AI-generated suggestions; critically evaluate them and ensure they align with your design goals and ethical principles.
- **Maintaining Creative Control:** AI is a powerful tool, but it should not replace human creativity. Use AI to augment your design process, not to automate it entirely. The final design decisions should always lie with the human designer.

By embracing AI responsibly and ethically, we can harness its power to create exceptional and inclusive user experiences for web and mobile platforms. The future of design is a collaborative one, where human creativity and AI intelligence work together to push the boundaries of what's possible.

CHAPTER 10 SUMMARY: UNLEASHING THE POWER OF AI FOR WEB AND MOBILE DESIGN

This chapter explored the exciting potential of Artificial Intelligence (AI) integration within Photoshop 2024, empowering you to design for the future of web and mobile experiences.

AI-powered Design for Responsive Layouts:

- We discussed AI-powered layout suggestions, a revolutionary feature that analyzes your design and generates optimal layouts for various screen sizes, saving you time and effort in the responsive design process.
- You learned how to potentially access and utilize these AI suggestions within Photoshop 2024, including specifying screen sizes and reviewing AI-generated variations.
- We highlighted the importance of using AI suggestions as a starting point, allowing you to incorporate your creative vision and ensure a cohesive user experience across all devices.

Enhancing Adaptive Design with AI:

- The chapter delved into how AI can augment your adaptive design workflow, where you create specific layouts for different device categories.
- We explored functionalities like Smart Object creation for easier variations across layouts, AI-powered content optimization for images and text, and context-aware design variations for portrait and landscape orientations on mobile devices.
- By combining AI suggestions with your creative control, you can achieve highly optimized and user-centric experiences across various devices.

User-Centered Design Informed by AI Analytics:

- This section highlighted the power of AI-powered user analytics, allowing you to analyze user behavior patterns and understand how users interact with your designs directly within Photoshop 2024.
- We discussed how AI can analyze web analytics data to identify areas where users might face difficulties, enabling you to make data-driven decisions to improve the overall user experience.
- By leveraging AI insights, you can move beyond guesswork and design interfaces that are not only aesthetically pleasing but also intuitive and meet the needs of your users.

Optimizing Design Workflows with AI Automation:

- The chapter explored how AI can streamline your design process by automating repetitive tasks. We discussed potential AI-powered tools within Photoshop 2024, including:
    - AI-powered background removal for isolating objects with impressive accuracy.
    - Smart Object manipulation with AI for intelligent resizing or adjustments while maintaining visual integrity.
    - AI-assisted content generation for creating placeholder content like stock images or lorem ipsum text.
- By identifying repetitive tasks and utilizing AI automation tools, you can dedicate more time and energy to the creative aspects of design.

A Glimpse into the Future of AI-powered Web and Mobile Design:

- We concluded the chapter by exploring emerging AI technologies that could revolutionize web and mobile design, such as AI-driven design inspiration, personalized UI design, voice-controlled design tools, and AI-powered accessibility checks.

- The future holds exciting possibilities for AI and human collaboration in design, pushing the boundaries of what's possible.

Responsible and Ethical Use of AI in Design:

- The chapter emphasized the importance of considering the ethical implications of AI implementation.
- We discussed potential biases within AI algorithms and the need for responsible use of AI tools, ensuring design suggestions align with your design goals and ethical principles.
- Human creativity should always be at the forefront, with AI acting as a powerful collaborator to enhance, not replace, the design process.

You can design exceptional and inclusive user experiences for web and mobile platforms, shaping the future of design by embracing AI as a valuable tool and adhering to responsible practices.

Review Questions

1. Explain the concept of AI-powered layout suggestions within Photoshop 2024. How can you utilize this feature to streamline the responsive design process for a website?
2. How can AI functionalities within Photoshop 2024, such as Smart Object manipulation and AI-powered content generation, be leveraged to enhance an adaptive design workflow?
3. The chapter discusses the ethical considerations surrounding AI use in design. Identify two potential risks associated with AI-powered design suggestions and explain how designers can mitigate these risks.

CHAPTER 11: MASTERING PHOTOSHOP 2024: ADVANCED TECHNIQUES AND BEST PRACTICES

Are you ready to unlock the full potential of the latest iteration of Photoshop? This chapter equips you with the knowledge and skills to navigate its intricacies and transform your design workflow. Whether you're a seasoned Photoshop user or eager to delve deeper into advanced techniques, this comprehensive guide will propel you forward.

We'll begin by conquering the new frontier: **exploring the updated Photoshop interface**. You'll become familiar with the latest layout, discover how to personalize your workspace for optimal efficiency, and master the functionalities of new or revamped tools within the toolbar.

Next, we embark on a journey into **advanced techniques for mastering image editing**. This section dives deep into non-destructive editing with layers and adjustment layers, unlocking the power of blending modes for creative effects. You'll master selective adjustments and masking techniques, and explore the potential of content-aware tools for seamless image manipulation.

The art of **professional retouching** is unveiled, revealing the secrets used by industry professionals. You'll learn frequency separation for flawless skin retouching, leverage dodge and burn techniques for precise light and shadow control, and discover advanced methods for retouching eyes and teeth. Additionally, we'll explore creative color grading techniques to establish a specific mood or style within your images.

For those who dream of creating surreal imagery, we delve into **the art of compositing**. This section equips you with the skills to make precise cutouts using selection and masking techniques. You'll learn how to match lighting and color for seamless integration, master advanced blending techniques for realistic compositions, and utilize dodge and burn to add depth and dimension.

But wait, there's more! We'll also unleash the power of **hidden gems: lesser-known features and shortcuts**. This section explores scripting and automation for streamlining repetitive tasks, utilizing Lens Blur for realistic depth effects, selective sharpening for targeted clarity enhancement, and valuable keyboard shortcuts to significantly improve your editing speed.

Finally, to solidify your newfound knowledge, we'll present **real-world mastery: professional editing case studies**. By following along with these step-by-step breakdowns, you'll witness professional retouching workflows used in high-fashion editorials and delve into the process of creating a dreamy landscape composite.

So, grab your digital pen or mouse, and prepare to embark on a journey to mastering Photoshop 2024. Let's unlock your creative potential and achieve professional-grade editing results!

11.1 Conquering the New Frontier: Exploring the Updated Photoshop Interface

This section equips you with the knowledge to navigate the latest interface with ease, ensuring you can leverage its full potential.

Here's what we'll be exploring:

- **Navigating the Workspace:** We'll begin by familiarizing ourselves with the updated layout and organization of tools within Photoshop 2024. You'll learn about the placement of panels, menus, and tools, understanding how they've been reorganized or revamped for optimal workflow.
- **Customizing Your Workspace:** This section empowers you to personalize your workspace for maximum efficiency. We'll explore creating custom panels to group frequently used tools together, along with saving and switching between different workspace layouts tailored to specific editing tasks. Additionally, you'll discover how to assign keyboard shortcuts to your favorite tools and actions, significantly boosting your editing speed.
- **Mastering the Updated Toolbar:** The ever-evolving toolbar holds some new or revamped tools. We'll delve into their functionalities and how they can enhance your design process. This could involve exploring new filters, adjustment tools, or selection techniques introduced in Photoshop 2024.

By conquering the new interface, you'll establish a solid foundation for mastering the advanced techniques and hidden gems explored in the following sections of this chapter. Let's dive in and get you comfortable within the latest iteration of Photoshop!

11.1.1 Navigating the Workspace in Photoshop 2024
Understanding the Workspace

Photoshop 2024 offers a powerful and versatile workspace where you can create, edit, and enhance your digital images. Familiarizing yourself with the key components will significantly boost your productivity. Let's explore:

1. **Opening an Image**:

- Launch **Photoshop 2024**.
- Choose **File → Open** to open an image in the workspace.
- The image will appear on the canvas.

2. **Canvas and Image Information**:
   - The **canvas** is the editable area where your image appears.
   - Look at the **status bar** for essential information about your image, such as dimensions, resolution, and color mode.
   - To examine details more closely, **zoom in** by pressing Ctrl + Spacebar and clicking where you want to magnify. Zoom out with Alt + Spacebar and clicking.

3. **Tool Options Panel**:
   - Located below the image window.
   - Displays options specific to the currently selected tool.
   - Easily switch between tool options by making choices in this panel.

4. **Toolbox (Tools Panel)**:
   - Found on the left side of the screen.
   - Contains various tools for tasks like selecting, painting, retouching, and more.
   - Click on a tool to activate it.

5. **Project Tabs**:
   - Represent open documents.
   - Switch between different projects by clicking the corresponding tab.

6. **Layers Panel** (Expert Mode):
   - Essential for working with layers.
   - Allows you to organize and manipulate different elements of your image.
   - Access it via **Window → Layers**.

11.1.2 Crafting Your Ideal Workspace: A Guide to Customization in Photoshop 2024

The default workspace in Photoshop 2024 might be a good starting point, but for true efficiency, customization is key. This section equips you with the tools to personalize your workspace to fit your specific editing style and needs.

Understanding the Interface Components:

Before diving into customization, let's gain a clear understanding of the key workspace components:

- **Canvas:** The central area is your canvas, where your image is displayed. This is where the magic happens as you edit and manipulate your photos.
- **Panels (Right-hand side):** These docked windows contain various tools and functionalities crucial for your editing process. Some core panels include Layers, Channels, Tools, and Properties. You can customize which panels are displayed based on your workflow.
- **Toolbox (Left-hand side):** This vertical bar houses a variety of tools for editing tasks like selection, cropping, painting, and retouching.

Explore the toolbox to discover the functionalities offered by each tool.
- **Option Bar (Top):** Context-sensitive, the Option Bar displays settings relevant to the currently selected tool or object within your image. These settings allow you to fine-tune the behavior of the tool and achieve your desired editing effects.
- **Menu Bar (Top):** The menu bar provides access to various program functions categorized by menus like File, Edit, Image, and Filter. Utilize these menus to manage your files, perform global edits, and access advanced functionalities.

Personalizing Your Workspace for Efficiency:

Now that you're familiar with the interface components, let's explore the power of customization:

- **Docking and Arranging Panels:** Panels can be dragged and docked to various locations within the workspace. Create a two-monitor setup and arrange panels on a secondary monitor for easy access while keeping your image centered on the primary monitor.
- **Creating Custom Panels:** Group frequently used tools together by creating custom panels. For instance, if you often use specific adjustment layers for retouching, you can create a custom panel containing only those adjustment layers for quick access.
- **Choosing a Color Scheme (Optional):** While not directly impacting efficiency, a color scheme that suits your preferences can enhance your editing experience. Go to **Menu > Photoshop > Preferences > Interface** to select your preferred color theme. Experiment with different shades to find what's most comfortable for your eyes.
- **Optimizing the Toolbar:** Streamline your toolbar by removing tools you rarely use. Drag and drop tools to rearrange them based on your most frequent workflow. This allows for quicker access to the tools you rely on the most.

- **Customizing Keyboard Shortcuts:** Keyboard shortcuts are a powerful way to expedite your workflow. Photoshop 2024 allows you to assign keyboard shortcuts to your favorite tools and actions. Go to **Edit > Keyboard Shortcuts** to set them up. This can significantly reduce the time spent navigating menus and toolbars, allowing you to focus on creative editing.

Saving Your Customized Workspace:

Once you've created a personalized layout that suits your workflow, save it as a custom workspace. This allows you to easily switch between different workspaces depending on the editing task at hand. For example, you might have a separate workspace optimized for photo editing with specific panels like Camera Raw and Curves readily available.

Here's how to save your workspace:

1. Go to the **Window** menu.
2. Select **Workspace** and then **New Workspace**.
3. Give your workspace a descriptive name and click **Save**.

Keeping It Neat:

A clutter-free workspace fosters productivity. Here are some tips for maintaining a clean and organized environment:

- **Utilize features like grouping layers and collapsing panels** to reduce visual clutter and focus on the specific area you're editing.
- **Close unnecessary documents** to free up screen space and avoid distractions.

By effectively customizing your workspace and utilizing keyboard shortcuts, you'll transform Photoshop into a personalized editing environment that caters to your specific workflow. This can significantly boost your editing speed and efficiency, allowing you to focus on the creative aspects of image manipulation.

11.1.3 Mastering the Updated Toolbar in Photoshop 2024 with Powerful New Features

The toolbar in Photoshop 2024 remains your command center, providing quick access to essential editing tools. This section equips you to leverage its potential, including exciting new functionalities introduced in this version.

Understanding the Toolbar:

The toolbar is typically located on the left side of the workspace. It contains a collection of icons representing various editing tools. Hovering your mouse cursor over an icon reveals a tooltip that displays the tool's name and a brief description of its function.

Exploring New and Revamped Tools:

- **Improved Remove Tool:**

The familiar Remove Tool has received an upgrade! You can now loop your selection around an object you want to remove instead of painstakingly brushing over its entire area. Photoshop 2024's magic lies in its ability to intelligently analyze the surrounding area and seamlessly fill in the gap left behind by the removed object. This significantly streamlines your workflow, especially when dealing with unwanted elements in your photos.

- **Lens Blur (Camera Raw):** Introducing a powerful new tool for photographers within Camera Raw! The Lens Blur filter allows you to apply a realistic blur effect to your photos, mimicking the bokeh created by real camera lenses. You can adjust the blur amount, choose from various bokeh shapes (like circular, elliptical, or polygonal) to achieve different aesthetic effects, and define the focal range to control which parts of your image remain sharp. This empowers you to create professional-looking depth-of-field effects within Photoshop 2024.

How to access:

1. Go to the **Filter** menu.
2. Choose **Camera Raw**.

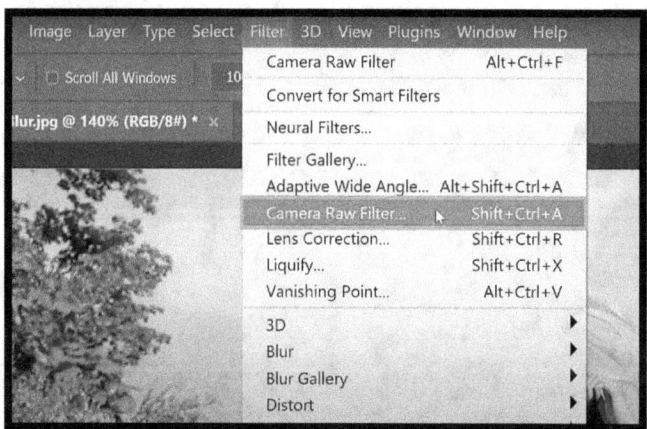

3. In the **Lens Blur panel**, you'll find the Lens Blur settings.

4. Click the **Apply** box to see the effect.

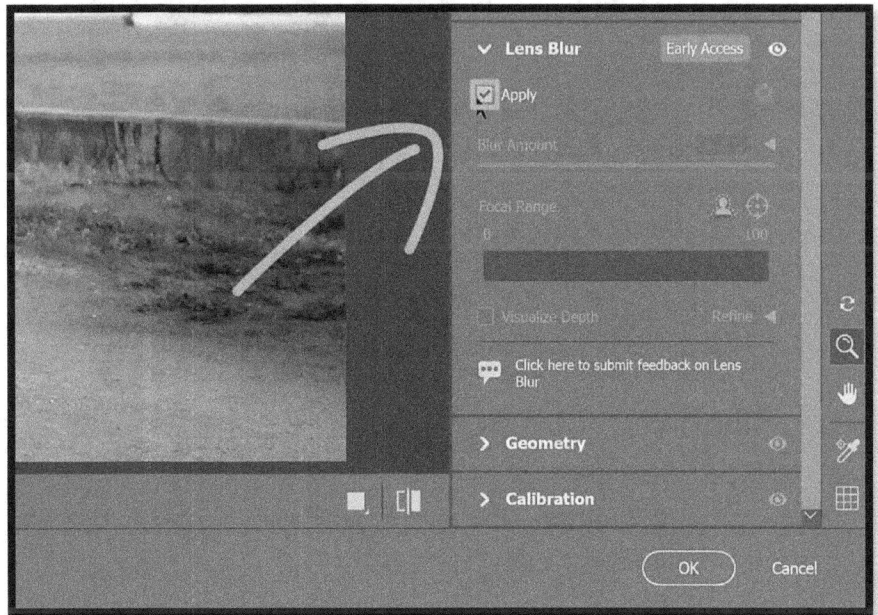

5. Adjust the **Blur Amount** slider to control the intensity of the blur.
6. You can also choose your preferred **bokeh style**.

Parametric Filters (Beta): Calling all creative explorers! Photoshop 2024 introduces a new set of non-destructive filters available under the Filter menu in beta testing. These include artistic effects like Oil Painting, Glitch for a vintage digital malfunction look, and Scratch Photo to create a worn-out film aesthetic. Each filter offers adjustable sliders, allowing you to experiment and create unique effects that enhance your image's mood and style. Here's how to access them:

1. **Open Photoshop 2024 Beta**: Launch Photoshop on your computer.
2. **Navigate to the Filter Menu**: Click on the **Filter** menu located at the top of the screen.
3. **Explore the Parametric Filters**: Scroll down within the Filter menu to find the **Parametric Filters (Beta)** section. Click on it to reveal the available filters.

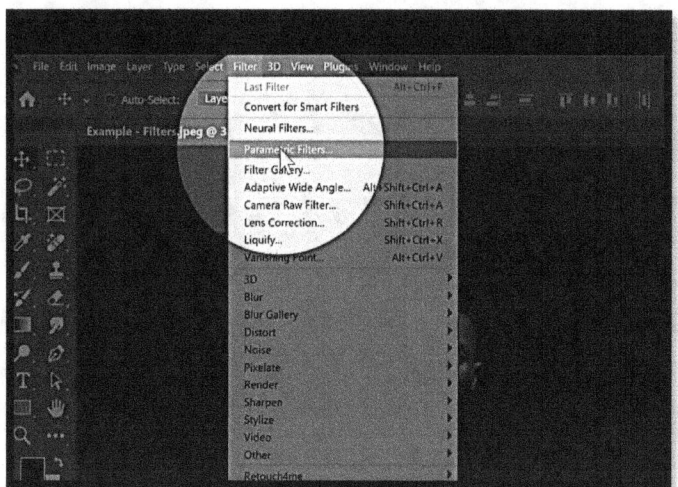

4. **Apply Filters**: Within the Parametric Filters section, you'll discover artistic effects such as:
    - **Oil Painting**: Transform your image into a beautiful oil painting.
    - **Glitch**: Achieve a vintage digital malfunction look.
    - **Scratch Photo**: Create a worn-out film aesthetic.

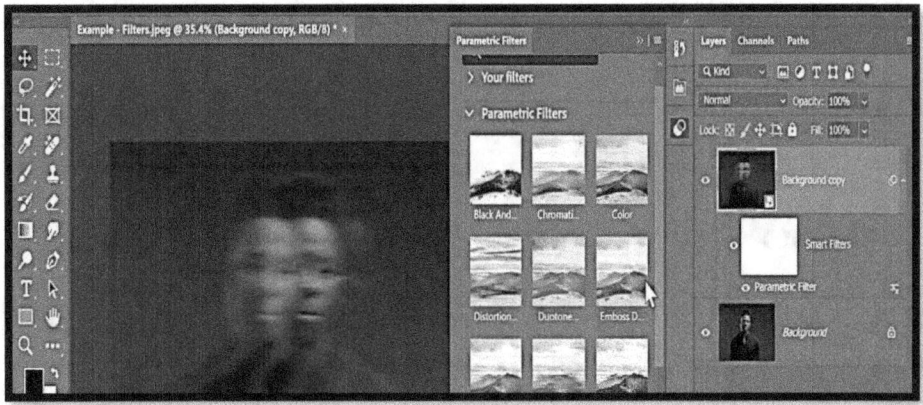

5. **Adjust the Sliders**: Each filter comes with adjustable sliders. Experiment with these sliders to fine-tune the effects and enhance your image's mood and style.

Mastering Core Toolbar Tools (Not affected by new features):

The core set of toolbar tools remains essential for building a solid foundation in image editing. (We can revisit this section in a future update if any core tools are revamped in later versions of Photoshop).

Effectively Utilizing the Toolbar:

- **Keyboard Shortcuts:** Assigning keyboard shortcuts to your most-used toolbar tools, including the new features, can significantly improve your editing speed. Explore the keyboard shortcut settings within Photoshop 2024 to personalize your workflow.
- **Tool Options and Contextual Menus:** Right-clicking on a toolbar tool often opens a contextual menu revealing additional options specific to that tool. Experiment with these options to discover the full range of functionalities offered by each tool, including the new features like the improved Remove Tool and Lens Blur options within Camera Raw.

By understanding the functionalities of the toolbar, incorporating the exciting new features of Photoshop 2024, and refining your skills with core tools, you'll transform it into a powerful instrument for executing your creative vision.

11.2.1 Non-Destructive Editing with Layers and Adjustment Layers:

The cornerstone of professional editing in Photoshop lies in non-destructive editing techniques. This approach allows you to experiment and make adjustments to your image without permanently altering the original data. Layers and adjustment layers are the building blocks for achieving this.

- **Layers:** Imagine layers as transparent sheets stacked upon each other. Each layer can contain a distinct element of your image, like the background, a foreground object, or text. You can edit each layer independently without affecting the others, offering immense flexibility.
- **Adjustment Layers:** These special layers don't contain image data themselves, but rather act as instructions that modify the underlying layers. Common adjustment layers include Levels for controlling brightness and contrast, Curves for fine-tuning tonal adjustments, and Hue/Saturation for manipulating color. The beauty lies in the fact that you can adjust these layers at any point without affecting the original image data.

11.2.2 Advanced Blending Modes: Unveiling the Magic of Layer Interactions

Blending modes, nestled within the layer panel in Photoshop 2024, act as the secret sauce for combining multiple layers and achieving captivating visual effects. By understanding how these modes interact, you'll unlock a world of creative possibilities.

Here's a glimpse into some popular blending modes and their applications:

- **Normal:** This is the default mode, where the upper layer simply replaces the underlying pixels.
- **Multiply:** This mode darkens the overall image. It's useful for creating shadows, adding depth, or darkening specific areas.
- **Screen:** Opposite to Multiply, Screen brightens the image. It's effective for lightening specific areas or creating a glowing effect.
- **Overlay:** This mode creates a contrasting effect, darkening darks and lightening lights. It's often used for adding texture or enhancing contrast.
- **Soft Light:** A subtler version of Overlay, Soft Light creates a more gradual lightening or darkening effect based on the underlying pixel intensity.
- **Color Burn:** This mode darkens the underlying layer based on the hue of the overlying layer. It's useful for adding shadows or color-specific darkening effects.
- **Color Dodge:** Conversely, Color Dodge brightens the underlying layer based on the hue of the overlying layer. It's effective for creating highlights or lightening specific color channels.

These are just a few examples, and Photoshop 2024 offers a plethora of blending modes to experiment with. We'll explore their functionalities in more detail through practical examples.

Beyond basic blending modes, you can unlock even greater creative potential by combining them with layer opacity and layer masks. Here's a peek at how these techniques can further enhance your edits:

- **Adjusting Layer Opacity:** Reducing the opacity of a layer allows the underlying layers to partially show through, creating a more subtle and nuanced effect.
- **Layer Masks:** Layer masks act like stencils, revealing or hiding portions of a layer. You can paint with black on a layer mask to hide

areas and white to reveal them, allowing for precise control over how blending modes interact with the underlying layers.

Mastering blending modes, layer opacity, and layer masks, provides you with the ability to create a vast array of visual effects, from subtle color adjustments to dramatic transformations.

11.2.3 Selective Adjustments and Masking: Unveiling the Art of Precise Editing

While adjustment layers offer powerful tools for global edits, selective adjustments and masking techniques empower you to target specific areas of your image for precise modifications. This section equips you with the skills to achieve professional-looking results by focusing adjustments on the elements that truly matter.

Accessing Selection Tools:

The foundation for selective adjustments lies in making precise selections. Here are some key selection tools in Photoshop 2024, and how to access them:

- **Marquee Tools (Rectangular, Elliptical, etc.):** These tools are located in the toolbar on the left side of the workspace. Look for the rectangular and elliptical icons, and a dropdown menu with additional marquee tool options.
- **Lasso Tool (Freehand and Polygonal):** Also located in the toolbar, the Lasso Tool is represented by a lasso icon. A second click on the icon reveals the Polygonal Lasso option.
- **Object Selection Tool (AI-powered):** This powerful tool utilizes artificial intelligence for automatic object selection. You'll find it within the toolbar under a rectangular marquee icon with a gear symbol in the corner. Clicking and holding on this icon reveals the Object Selection Tool option.

Utilizing Adjustment Layers for Selective Edits:

Once you've made a selection, you can leverage adjustment layers for targeted adjustments. Here's how to navigate to them:

1. Go to the **Layers** panel (usually located on the right side of the workspace).
2. Click on the **Create a new adjustment layer** icon (looks like a black and white half-filled circle at the bottom of the panel).
3. Choose the desired adjustment layer from the menu (e.g., Levels, Curves, Hue/Saturation).

Creating Selective Adjustments with Clipping Masks:

1. With your selection active, create a new adjustment layer as described above.
2. Hold down the **Alt** key (Option key on Mac) and click between the adjustment layer and the image layer in the Layers panel. This clips the adjustment layer to the selection, ensuring edits only affect the selected pixels.

Creating Selective Adjustments with Layer Masks:

1. Create a new adjustment layer as described above.
2. Click on the adjustment layer to activate it.
3. Click on the **Add layer mask** icon at the bottom of the Layers panel (looks like a rectangle with a circle inside).
4. Use the brush tool (located in the toolbar) to paint with black on the mask to hide the adjustment in specific areas, and white to reveal it.

Exploring Advanced Masking Techniques:

Masking techniques extend beyond basic black and white painting. Here are some additional methods to refine your selections, all accessible within the Layers panel:

- **Feathering:** Right-click on your selection and choose **Feather** from the context menu. Adjust the feather radius to soften the selection edges.
- **Refine Edge:** With your selection active, go to **Select > Refine Edge**. This powerful tool allows for precise adjustments to the selection based on various properties.
- **Gradient Masks:** Click on the mask thumbnail next to your adjustment layer to activate the mask. Choose the **Gradient tool** (located in the toolbar) and define your gradient (e.g., black to white for a vignette) to create a smooth transition between adjusted and unadjusted areas.

11.2.4 Content-Aware Tools: Unleashing the Power of AI-Assisted Editing

The latest versions of Photoshop boast powerful content-aware tools that leverage artificial intelligence to streamline your editing workflow and achieve impressive results. This section delves into the functionalities of two key tools: Content-Aware Fill and the Healing Brush, empowering you to seamlessly manipulate images and remove unwanted elements.

Content-Aware Fill:

Imagine having the ability to remove an object from your image and have Photoshop intelligently fill the gap with a background that seamlessly blends in. That's the magic of Content-Aware Fill! Here's how to use it:

1. **Make your selection:** Use the selection tools we discussed in the previous section (11.2.3) to carefully select the object you want to remove.
2. **Navigate to Content-Aware Fill:** Go to the **Edit** menu at the top of the workspace. Select **Fill** from the dropdown menu.
3. **Content-Aware Options:** In the Fill window that appears, choose **Content-Aware** from the Contents dropdown menu. You'll also find options to define how the fill analyzes the surrounding area (e.g., Content Aware, Content Aware Scale) to achieve the most natural-looking results.
4. **Click OK:** Photoshop will analyze the surrounding area and intelligently fill the gap left behind by your selection.

Healing Brush:

The Healing Brush acts like a magic wand for removing blemishes, imperfections, or unwanted objects in a more targeted manner. Here's how to wield it:

1. **Activate the Healing Brush:** Find the Healing Brush tool within the toolbar (typically represented by a band-aid icon).
2. **Sampling Source:** Hold down the **Alt** key (Option key on Mac) and click on a clean area near the imperfection you want to remove. This defines the sampling source, the area Photoshop uses to borrow texture from.
3. **Brush over the imperfection:** While holding down the Alt/Option key, carefully brush over the imperfection you want to remove. Photoshop will seamlessly blend the texture from the sampling source to cover the unwanted element.
4. **Adjust brush size and settings (Optional):** The brush options bar at the top of the workspace allows you to adjust the size and hardness of the brush for optimal control. You can also experiment with additional settings like Content Aware to achieve more natural-looking results.

By mastering Content-Aware Fill and the Healing Brush, you'll gain the ability to:

- Remove unwanted objects from your photos, like power lines or distracting background elements.
- Retouch blemishes, imperfections, or dust spots for a clean and polished look.
- Creatively manipulate backgrounds or extend image elements seamlessly.

11.3 Professional Retouching: Unveiling the Secrets of the Masters

The art of professional retouching goes beyond basic blemish removal. It's about enhancing natural beauty, creating a specific mood or style, and achieving a flawless, polished final product. This section equips you with the essential techniques and tools to retouch portraits like a pro in Photoshop 2024.

Frequency Separation for Flawless Skin Retouching:

A cornerstone technique in professional retouching is frequency separation. This process involves separating the image's detail (high frequency) from its color and texture (low frequency). Here's a simplified breakdown:

1. **Duplicate your image layer.**
2. **Apply a High Pass filter:** This filter allows you to control the high-frequency detail. Adjust the filter amount to isolate skin texture without affecting color.
3. **Change the blending mode to Soft Light:** This creates a smooth separation between the detail and texture layers.
4. **Edit the high-frequency layer:** Use tools like the Healing Brush or dodge and burn (covered later) to smoothen blemishes and refine skin texture while preserving natural details like pores and wrinkles.

By mastering frequency separation, you'll gain the ability to achieve natural-looking skin retouching that avoids the dreaded "plasticky" effect.

Dodge and Burn for Precise Light and Shadow Control:

Dodge and burn are fundamental techniques for enhancing light and shadow in your image. Here's a basic understanding:

- **Dodge (Lighten):** Use a brush tool with a low opacity and exposure to lighten specific areas, like brightening shadows under the eyes or adding a catchlight to the eyes.
- **Burn (Darken):** Use a brush tool with a low opacity to darken specific areas, such as sculpting facial features or adding depth to the image.

By mastering dodge and burn techniques, you can refine facial features, enhance dimension, and create a more polished look.

Advanced Techniques for Eyes and Teeth:

The eyes and teeth are focal points in a portrait. Professional retouchers dedicate special attention to these areas. Here's a glimpse into some techniques:

- **Eye Retouching:** Subtly sharpen the iris for added clarity, whiten the whites of the eyes for a refreshed look, and use dodge and burn to enhance depth and definition.
- **Teeth Whitening:** Use selective adjustments or layer masks to target the teeth for a natural-looking whitening effect, avoiding an overly bright or unnatural appearance.

Creative Color Grading for Mood and Style:

Color grading isn't just for movies! It's a powerful tool for establishing a specific mood or style in your portraits. Here's how to explore creative color grading:

1. **Create a Selective Color adjustment layer:** This allows you to target specific color ranges within your image.

2. **Adjust color sliders:** Experiment with adjusting the Neutrals, Reds, Yellows, and other color sliders to create a warm, cool, vintage, or other desired aesthetic effect.

11.4 Compositing: Mastering the Art of Creating Surreal Imagery

In this section (11.4), we delve into the art of compositing in Photoshop 2024, equipping you with the skills to seamlessly combine multiple images into fantastical or realistic compositions.

Understanding the Fundamentals of Compositing:

Compositing involves selecting elements from different images and combining them into a single, cohesive final piece. It's a technique used extensively in professional photography, advertising, and even blockbuster movies. Here's a breakdown of the key steps involved:

1. **Concept and Planning:** Before diving into Photoshop, take some time to brainstorm your creative vision. Sketch thumbnails or create mood boards to visualize your final composition.
2. **Source Image Selection:** Choose high-resolution images that complement each other in terms of lighting, perspective, and color. Consider factors like focus distance and shadows to ensure a believable final outcome.
3. **Making Precise Cutouts:** This is where your selection skills come into play (refer back to Section 11.2.3 for a refresher). Utilize selection tools, masking techniques, and the Refine Edge tool (introduced in Section 11.2.3) to achieve clean and precise cutouts of your desired elements.

Seamless Integration: Matching Lighting and Color:

Once you have your cutouts, the key lies in making them appear as if they naturally belong in the same scene. Here's how to achieve seamless integration:

- **Levels and Curves Adjustments:** Fine-tune the brightness, contrast, and overall color tone of your cutout elements to match the lighting and color of the background image.
- **Color Matching Tools:** Explore tools like Match Color in Photoshop 2024 to analyze and adjust the color properties of your cutout elements to seamlessly blend with the background.
- **Layer Blending Modes:** Experiment with blending modes (covered in Section 11.2.2) to further refine how the cutout element interacts with the background lighting and color.

Adding Realism: Shadows and Depth:

Creating a convincing composite requires establishing a sense of depth and realism. Here are some techniques to achieve this:

- **Drop Shadows:** Add realistic drop shadows beneath your cutout elements to simulate their interaction with the background surface.
- **Adjustment Layers for Shadows and Highlights:** Create adjustment layers (Levels, Curves) specifically for adding subtle shadows or highlights to your cutout elements, further integrating them into the scene.
- **Perspective Adjustments:** The Transform tools in Photoshop 2024 allow you to adjust the perspective of your cutout elements to perfectly match the perspective of the background image.

11.5 Unleashing the Hidden Gems: Lesser-Known Features and Shortcuts in Photoshop 2024

While we've explored some core functionalities in Photoshop 2024, there's a treasure trove of hidden gems waiting to be unearthed! This section (11.5) delves into lesser-known features and shortcuts that can significantly enhance your editing workflow and open doors to creative possibilities.

1. Scripting and Automation: Batch Editing Made Easy

Imagine applying the same edit to a hundred photos with just a few clicks! Scripting in Photoshop 2024 allows you to automate repetitive tasks. While scripting might sound advanced, there are user-friendly options to explore:

- **Actions Panel:** Record a series of steps you take to edit an image (like resizing and applying a filter). Then, you can play back this action on multiple images at once, saving you tremendous time and effort.
- **Batch Commands:** For more basic repetitive tasks, explore the Batch Commands feature. You can instruct Photoshop to perform the same edit (like resizing or converting file formats) on a group of images simultaneously.

2. Selective Sharpening: Targeting Clarity Where You Need It

Sharpening an entire image can sometimes introduce unwanted noise. Selective sharpening allows you to focus on specific areas that require clarity enhancement. Here's how:

- Make a selection of the area you want to sharpen.
- Apply the Sharpen filter (Filter > Sharpen).
- Adjust the amount of sharpening to enhance clarity without introducing noise.

3. Keyboard Shortcuts: The Language of Efficiency

Keyboard shortcuts are your gateway to editing mastery in Photoshop 2024. Learning a few key shortcuts can significantly accelerate your workflow. Here are some essentials to get you started:

- **Tool Shortcuts:** Most tools in the toolbar have keyboard shortcuts (listed in the tooltip when you hover over the tool icon). Utilize shortcuts for frequently used tools like the Crop Tool (C), Brush Tool (B), and Eraser Tool (E).
- **Basic Editing Shortcuts:** Save time with shortcuts like Copy (Ctrl/Cmd + C), Paste (Ctrl/Cmd + V), and Undo (Ctrl/Cmd + Z).
- **Customizing Shortcuts:** Photoshop 2024 allows you to personalize your workspace by assigning custom shortcuts to your favorite functions. Explore the Edit > Keyboard Shortcuts menu to discover this power!

11.6 Professional Editing Case Studies: Witnessing the Mastery in Action

Here, we'll transition from theory to practice by exploring professional editing case studies in Photoshop 2024. Witnessing the step-by-step workflows used by industry professionals will solidify your understanding of the techniques covered throughout this chapter and inspire you to achieve exceptional results in your own edits.

Case Study 1: High-Fashion Editorial Retouching

Imagine transforming a raw fashion photograph into a captivating image for a high-end magazine spread. This case study will unveil the retouching techniques used by professionals to achieve a flawless, polished look:

- **Frequency separation for natural-looking skin retouching.** (We explored this technique in Section 11.3)

- **Dodge and burn for precise sculpting of facial features and adding depth.** (Covered in Section 11.3)
- **Selective adjustments for enhancing specific color channels, like brightening clothing or adding vibrancy to makeup.** (A technique we touched upon in Section 11.2.3)
- **Liquify filter for subtle body contouring (optional).** This powerful tool allows for non-destructive adjustments to body shapes, but should be used with a light touch to maintain a realistic aesthetic.

Case Study 2: Dreamy Landscape Composite

Have you ever dreamt of creating a fantastical landscape by combining elements from different photographs? This case study will guide you through the compositing process:

- **Planning and selecting high-resolution source images with compatible lighting and color.** (Discussed in Section 11.4)
- **Utilizing selection tools, masking techniques, and Refine Edge for achieving clean cutouts of desired elements.** (Refer back to Sections 11.2.3 and 11.4 for a refresher)
- **Matching lighting and color of cutout elements to seamlessly blend with the background image using Levels, Curves adjustments, and potentially Color Matching tools.** (Covered in Section 11.4)
- **Adding realistic shadows and depth using techniques like drop shadows and adjustment layers for shadows and highlights.** (Explored in Section 11.4)

By following these step-by-step breakdowns and exploring the thought processes behind each professional edit, you'll gain valuable insights into how to translate theory into practice within Photoshop 2024.

Summary

This chapter provided a comprehensive guide to mastering Photoshop 2024. You learned how to navigate the updated interface, conquer advanced editing techniques, and achieve professional-looking edits.

The chapter covered essential tools for non-destructive editing, the power of blending modes for creative effects, and professional retouching secrets like frequency separation and dodge and burn.

You also learned about creating surreal imagery through compositing, mastering selection and masking techniques, and adding depth through shadows and perspective manipulation.

Hidden gems like scripting for automation, Lens Blur for realistic depth effects, and selective sharpening were also explored. Finally, the chapter solidified your knowledge with professional editing case studies in high-fashion retouching and dreamy landscape composites.

Review Questions

1. Explain the concept of non-destructive editing and discuss two tools explored in the chapter that enable this type of editing in Photoshop 2024.

2. Beyond basic adjustments, describe two advanced techniques covered in the chapter that can be used to achieve professional-looking retouching.

3. The chapter explores the art of compositing. Briefly outline the key steps involved in creating a seamless composite image in Photoshop 2024.

CHAPTER 12: ADVANCED IMAGE EDITING TECHNIQUES: PUSHING THE BOUNDARIES

Throughout Chapter 11, you embarked on a journey to master the essential tools and techniques in Photoshop 2024. Now, it's time to break free from the ordinary and delve into the world of pushing creative boundaries.

This chapter equips you with advanced editing skills that will elevate your projects to a whole new level. We'll revisit and refine foundational techniques, explore complex workflows for photo manipulation and compositing, and unlock the power of advanced masking and blending to achieve seamless integration.

Remember, the key to mastering advanced editing lies in experimentation and embracing the unknown. This chapter provides the springboard; your creativity and exploration will propel you further.

Are you ready to redefine the limits of what's possible with your images? Let's dive in!

12.1.1 Frequency Separation Mastery: Refining Skin Texture Control

Remember the magic of frequency separation from Chapter 11.3? We separated the image's detail (high frequency) from its color and texture (low frequency) for flawless skin retouching. Now, let's push this technique even further!

High-Pass Filter Finesse:

The High-Pass filter remains our gateway to isolating high-frequency detail. But this time, we'll explore the impact of different blend modes on the final outcome. Here's how:

1. Duplicate your image layer and apply a High-Pass filter.
2. Experiment with blend modes: Instead of just Soft Light, try using Overlay or even Lighten blend modes. Each offers a distinct effect on the high-frequency detail. Overlay creates a more intense contrast, while Lighten can be useful for removing minor blemishes.
3. Adjust filter strength: Remember, the High-Pass filter amount controls the amount of detail extracted. Play with the filter strength in conjunction with different blend modes to achieve the perfect balance between smoothing texture and preserving natural skin features.

Beyond Soft Light: Exploring Blend Mode Options

Soft Light might be our initial go-to blend mode, but venturing beyond opens doors to artistic expression:

- **Overlay:** This mode intensifies the underlying texture while preserving some highlights. It's great for removing minor imperfections and adding a bit of skin definition.
- **Lighten:** Want to tackle stubborn blemishes or dark circles? Lighten mode selectively lightens areas in the high-frequency layer, allowing you to target imperfections for a cleaner look. Remember, use a low opacity to avoid an unnatural, bleached appearance.

12.1.2 Advanced Dodge and Burn: Sculpting with Light and Shadow

We explored the basic principles of dodge and burn in Chapter 11.3 for light and shadow control. Now, buckle up as we delve into advanced methods used by professional retouchers to truly sculpt and enhance facial features.

Dodge and Burn: Beyond the Basic Brush

While the brush tool remains our primary weapon, professional retouchers leverage additional techniques for targeted adjustments:

- **Channel Targeting:** Dodge and burn adjustments can be applied to specific color channels (Red, Green, Blue) within your image. This allows for highly precise control. For example, dodging the red channel brightens areas like lips, while burning the red channel reduces redness in blemishes.
- **Mixer Brush Mastery:** The Mixer Brush offers incredible control over color and saturation while dodging and burning. Sample a neutral skin tone from your image and use the Mixer Brush to subtly reduce unwanted redness or add a touch of warmth to specific areas.

Channel Targeting in Action:

1. Go to the Channels panel and select a specific color channel (e.g., Red for targeting blemishes).
2. Create a copy of that channel.
3. Use the Dodge or Burn tool (adjusted to a low opacity) to target adjustments specifically within that color channel. Burning on the red channel reduces redness, while dodging brightens areas like lips.

Mixer Brush Magic:

1. Sample a neutral skin tone from your image using the Eyedropper tool.
2. Select the Mixer Brush tool and adjust its brush settings (size, opacity) for precise control.
3. With the sampled neutral tone loaded in the Mixer Brush, paint over areas with unwanted redness to subtly reduce it. You can also use the Mixer Brush to add a touch of warmth to specific areas by sampling a slightly warmer skin tone.

12.1.3 Portrait Sculpting with Liquify: The Art of Subtlety

Portrait retouching isn't just about blemishes; professional retouchers can subtly sculpt facial features to enhance their natural beauty. Here's where the Liquify tool, briefly mentioned in Chapter 11.6, comes into play. We'll explore techniques for achieving natural-looking portrait sculpting without venturing into caricature territory.

Liquify Responsibly: Maintaining Realism

The Liquify tool is powerful, but overuse can lead to distorted and unrealistic results. Here's the key: subtlety!

1. **Duplicate your image layer.** This creates a non-destructive base for your sculpting work.
2. **Navigate to Filter > Liquify.** Enter the Liquify workspace.
3. **Zoom in for precision:** Use the zoom tool to focus on specific facial areas you want to sculpt.

Targeted Adjustments for Natural Enhancement

Let's explore some sculpting techniques for common areas:

- **Jawline Definition:** Use the Forward Warp tool (looks like a pushpin) to subtly push in along the jawline, creating a more defined look. Remember, small adjustments are key!
- **Chin Enhancement:** For a slightly stronger chin, use the Push Up tool (looks like an upside-down teardrop) to gently lift the central area of the chin.
- **Eye Widening (Optional):** While exercising caution to avoid uncanny valley effects, the Expand tool (looks like an outward arrow) can be used very subtly to slightly widen the space between the eyes, creating a more alert look.

Note: The goal is to enhance natural beauty, not reshape the face entirely. Use a light touch and take breaks to compare your adjustments to the original image to avoid going overboard.

12.2 Complex Photo Manipulation and Compositing: Pushing the Boundaries of Reality

We've conquered retouching techniques, and now it's time to delve into the world of photo manipulation and compositing, where you can build fantastical scenes or seamlessly merge elements from different photographs. Buckle up, as we explore advanced selection and masking methods, unlock the potential of advanced cloning and healing tools, and dive into complex compositing workflows.

12.2.1 Advanced Selection and Masking Techniques: Precision is Key

Building a convincing composite relies on precise selection and masking of your source elements. Here, we'll build upon the foundation established in Chapter 11.2.3 and introduce advanced techniques for achieving pixel-perfect selections:

- **Color Range Selections:** This powerful tool allows you to isolate specific color elements within your image. Imagine selecting all the blue sky in a landscape photo with a single click!
- **Channel Masking:** Channels within your image hold information about color and luminosity. By learning to use channels as masks, you can achieve incredibly precise selections based on specific tonal or color values.

Color Range Selections in Action:

1. Go to the Select menu and choose Color Range.
2. Use the eyedropper tool to sample the color you want to select (e.g., blue sky).

3. Adjust the Fuzziness slider to refine the selection's edge, ensuring you capture the sky without grabbing unwanted foreground elements.

Channel Masking Magic:

1. Go to the Channels panel and identify a channel that best represents the area you want to select (e.g., the Blue channel might isolate the sky well).
2. Click the channel's name while holding down the Command/Ctrl key to create a selection based on that channel's information.

12.2.2 Advanced Cloning and Healing: Seamless Integration

Flawless compositing hinges on seamlessly integrating elements from different sources. We'll revisit familiar tools like the Healing Brush (introduced in Chapter 11.2.4) but delve deeper into advanced techniques for achieving undetectable results.

Beyond the Basic Healing Brush: Unveiling Powerful Tools

The Healing Brush is great for basic fixes, but for complex composites, we have advanced tools in our arsenal:

- **Patch Tool:** This content-aware tool excels at seamlessly replacing unwanted areas with content from another part of your image. Imagine removing a power line from a landscape photo by using the Patch Tool to copy a clean sky section over it.
- **Spot Healing Brush with Content Aware:** This enhanced version of the Healing Brush analyzes the surrounding image content and intelligently replaces imperfections while preserving texture and detail. It's ideal for removing dust spots or minor blemishes on objects within your composite.

Patch Tool Perfection:

1. Select the Patch Tool (looks like a bandaid).
2. Define the source area by dragging a selection around the content you want to use for the replacement (e.g., a clean sky section).
3. Drag the selection over the area you want to replace (e.g., the power line). Photoshop will intelligently blend the source area onto the target area, seamlessly removing the unwanted element.

Spot Healing Brush Mastery:

1. Select the Spot Healing Brush (looks like a Band-Aid with a target) and ensure "Content Aware" is selected in the options bar.
2. Set the brush size according to the imperfection you want to remove (e.g., dust spot).
3. Click on the imperfection. Photoshop will analyze the surrounding area and replace the blemish with matching texture and detail, creating a seamless fix.

12.2.3 Advanced Compositing Workflows: Orchestrating Reality

We've mastered the art of selection and seamless integration; now it's time to delve into the fascinating world of crafting complex composite imagery. Here, we'll transcend basic compositing techniques from Chapter 11.4 and explore workflows for creating elaborate lighting effects, incorporating 3D elements, and even achieving realistic motion blur within your composites.

Beyond Blending Modes: Complex Lighting Effects

Lighting is paramount to creating a believable composite. We'll move beyond basic blending modes and explore advanced techniques for manipulating light and shadow:

- **Layer Effects and Adjustment Layers:** Utilize tools like Drop Shadow, Outer Glow, and adjustment layers like Levels and Curves

to create realistic lighting effects on your composite elements. Imagine adding a subtle drop shadow to a bird you've composited into a scene, grounding it within the environment.
- **Matching Lighting with Adjustment Layers:** Light plays a crucial role in creating a cohesive composite. Use adjustment layers like Curves and Color Balance to meticulously match the lighting of your source elements to the background scene for a seamless blend.

Creating Depth with Lighting:

1. Add a drop shadow to your composited element (e.g., the bird) using the Layer Styles panel. Adjust the shadow properties like opacity, angle, and distance to create a sense of depth and separation from the background.
2. Utilize Curves or Color Balance adjustment layers to subtly adjust the color temperature and brightness of your composited element to better match the overall lighting of the background scene.

Bringing the Extraordinary to Life

We've explored crafting realistic lighting effects within composites. Now, let's push the boundaries even further by incorporating the magic of 3D elements!

3D Integration: A New Dimension in Compositing

Imagine placing a sleek spaceship into a breathtaking landscape or adding a photorealistic robot into your scene. 3D elements open doors to limitless creative possibilities. Here's a glimpse of what you'll learn:

- **Understanding 3D file formats:** We'll explore common 3D file formats like OBJ and FBX, used for importing 3D models into Photoshop.

- **Basic manipulation of 3D elements:** Learn how to position, rotate, and scale your 3D model within your composite using Photoshop's 3D manipulation tools.
- **Material application and lighting:** Discover how to apply textures and materials to your 3D model and manipulate lighting properties to seamlessly integrate it into your scene.

Importing and Positioning Your 3D Model:

1. Go to File > Open and locate your desired 3D model file (e.g., OBJ).
2. Within the Layers panel, you'll see your 3D model as a new layer. Use the Move tool to position it within your composite.
3. Utilize the 3D manipulation tools in the Options bar (located at the top of the workspace) to rotate and scale your 3D model to fit perfectly within your scene.

Material Magic and Lighting Control:

1. Double-click the 3D model layer thumbnail to access its properties panel.
2. Explore the material settings to apply textures and adjust surface properties like roughness and metallicity to achieve a realistic look for your 3D element.
3. Utilize lighting tools within Photoshop's 3D workspace to manipulate light direction, intensity, and shadows on your 3D model, ensuring it seamlessly interacts with the lighting of your background scene.

Refining Control with Advanced Masking

We've unveiled the magic of 3D elements in composites. Now, let's revisit masking, a fundamental concept in compositing (introduced in Chapter 11.2.3) and explore advanced techniques for achieving even more precise control over how image elements interact within your creation.

Beyond Basic Masks: Nested Masking Workflows

Imagine creating a composite where a bird with outstretched wings gracefully flies past a tree with leaves partially obscuring its body. Basic masks might not suffice for this level of detail. Nested masking workflows come to the rescue!

- **Creating Nested Masks:** This technique involves creating multiple masks within a single layer, allowing for highly specific control over how different parts of an element interact with the background.
- **Refined Transparency and Blending:** Nested masks offer the ability to define areas of partial transparency within your element, creating a more natural and believable interaction with the background.

Masking Magic with a Bird in Flight:

1. Create a mask on the bird layer, roughly outlining its shape.
2. Refine the mask using tools like the Brush tool to ensure clean edges around the bird's body.
3. Now, create a nested mask within the existing bird mask. This nested mask will focus on the bird's wings.
4. Use the Brush tool (with a lower opacity) on this nested mask to paint on areas where the bird's wings would be partially obscured by leaves in the background scene.

By creating nested masks, you've achieved a more refined level of control. The bird appears to naturally interact with the leaves, with some wing feathers showing partial transparency where they overlap the leaves.

Mastering Nested Masks Opens Doors:

This is just a glimpse of the power of nested masks. With practice, you can use them for complex tasks like creating realistic smoke effects or adding subtle shadows cast by one element onto another.

The Illusion of Movement with Matchmoving

Compositing isn't limited to static scenes. Let's delve into the fascinating world of matchmoving, a technique used to create realistic motion blur within your composites, making it appear as if elements are truly moving within the scene.

Matchmoving: Bringing Still Elements to Life

Imagine adding a speeding car with realistic motion blur into a city scene, or compositing a majestic dragon soaring through the sky with its wings leaving a trail of blurred motion. Matchmoving empowers you to achieve these effects.

- **Understanding Motion Paths:** This concept defines the trajectory along which an element will move within your composite.
- **Blur Filters and Customization:** We'll explore advanced blur filters like Motion Blur and how to customize them to achieve realistic motion blur effects based on the element's speed and direction.

Simulating Motion Blur with a Speeding Car:

1. Define a motion path for your car element within the Timeline panel. This path will dictate the car's movement within the scene.
2. Once the car is positioned and animated along the path, apply the Motion Blur filter to the car layer.
3. Adjust the blur angle within the Motion Blur filter properties to match the direction of the car's movement. Additionally, experiment with the blur distance to create the appropriate intensity of motion blur based on the car's perceived speed.

12.3 Mastering Masking and Blending for Flawless Integration

The magic of compositing lies in creating seamless transitions between elements, making them appear as if they naturally belong within the same scene. Mastering masking and blending techniques is the cornerstone of achieving this illusion. In this section, we'll revisit blending modes (introduced in Chapter 11.2.2) and explore their use in combination with adjustment layers for achieving complex and creative effects. Additionally, we'll delve into the power of nested masking workflows (introduced in 12.3.3) for even more precise control over how elements interact within your composite.

12.3.1 Advanced Blending Modes and Adjustments: Pushing Creative Boundaries

Blending modes are the backbone of controlling how image elements interact within a composite. We explored basic blending modes in Chapter 11.2.2, but here, we'll delve deeper and explore their use in combination with adjustment layers to unlock a world of creative possibilities.

- **Understanding Adjustment Layers:** These non-destructive layers allow you to globally adjust properties like color, brightness, and contrast within your composite, offering immense creative flexibility.
- **Creative Blending Mode Exploration:** We'll move beyond basic blending modes like Normal and Multiply and experiment with modes like Overlay, Soft Light, and Color Dodge to create unique visual effects and enhance specific aspects of your composite elements.

Unlocking Creative Potential with Adjustment Layers:

1. Create an adjustment layer (e.g., Curves, Color Balance) above your element layer within the Layers panel.
2. By adjusting the properties within the adjustment layer, you can globally affect the element below. For example, using a Curves adjustment layer with a specific S-curve can add a touch of vibrancy to your composited bird element.
3. Experiment with different blending modes for the adjustment layer itself. A Curves adjustment layer set to "Overlay" mode can subtly enhance the contrast and color within your bird element while preserving the overall lighting of the background scene.

12.3.2 Advanced Masking Workflows: Refining Control with Nested Masks

We touched upon the concept of nested masks in Section 12.3.3. Now, let's delve deeper into this powerful technique, unlocking an even greater degree of control over how elements interact within your composite.

Nested Masking Mastery: A World of Creative Possibilities

Nested masks allow you to create multiple masks within a single layer. Imagine a composite where a person is holding a bouquet of flowers. A basic mask might cut out the person, but what about the individual flowers within the bouquet? Nested masks come in!

- **Building Complex Masks:** We'll explore techniques for creating intricate nested masks to define areas of transparency and partial visibility within specific elements of your composite.
- **Achieving Realistic Interactions:** By mastering nested masks, you can create effects like wispy hair strands blending seamlessly behind a person's ear, or flower petals delicately overlapping one another, adding a depth of realism to your composites.

Creating Nested Masks for Realistic Flower Overlap:

1. Create a mask on the flower bouquet layer, roughly outlining its shape.
2. Refine the mask to ensure clean edges around the bouquet.
3. Now, create a nested mask within the existing bouquet mask. This nested mask will focus on the individual flowers.
4. Use the Brush tool (with a low opacity) on this nested mask to paint on areas where specific flower petals would overlap one another, creating a natural transparency effect.

By creating nested masks for the flowers, you've achieved a more realistic look. The individual flower petals interact with each other naturally, with some appearing partially obscured behind others.

Nested Masks: A Gateway to Advanced Compositing

This is just a starting point. With practice, you can use nested masks for fur, hair, smoke effects, and other scenarios requiring precise control over transparency and interaction between elements within your composite.

12.4 Color Grading and Tonal Adjustments: The Art of Professional Finishing

We've conquered the art of compositing and manipulating individual elements within your image. Now, let's explore the world of color grading and tonal adjustments, the magic touch that transforms a good composite into a professional-looking masterpiece.

12.4.1 The Power of Color Grading: Setting the Mood

Color grading isn't just about technical adjustments; it's about storytelling. By manipulating color tones and saturation, you can evoke specific moods and emotions within your viewers. Here, we'll explore color grading techniques used by professional editors to achieve various stylistic effects.

- **Understanding Color Wheels and Color Balance:** We'll revisit the fundamentals of color theory and delve into using color wheels and adjustment layers like Color Balance to achieve specific color palettes and moods within your composite.
- **Selective Color Grading:** Learn how to target and adjust specific color ranges within your composite, allowing you to fine-tune the look of individual elements or areas of the scene.

Color Grading for a Cinematic Look:

1. Go to the Color Balance adjustment layer and explore adjusting the shadows, midtones, and highlights. Shifting these towards cooler tones can create a more cinematic and professional look.
2. Utilize the Selective Color adjustment layer to target specific color ranges. For example, decreasing the saturation of yellows in a landscape composite can create a more subdued and calming atmosphere.

12.4.2 Tonal Adjustments: Refining Light and Shadow

Color grading sets the mood, but tonal adjustments fine-tune the overall light and shadow play within your composite, adding depth and realism. Here, we'll explore advanced adjustment layers and techniques used by professional editors to achieve mastery over light and shadow.

- **Dodge and Burn on Adjustment Layers:** We revisited dodge and burn tools in Chapter 12.2.2, but here, we'll explore using them on adjustment layers, allowing for non-destructive global adjustments to light and shadow across your composite.
- **Curves and Levels for Precision Control:** These powerful adjustment layers offer immense control over tonal values within your composite. Learn how to use them to manipulate brightness, contrast, and specific highlights and shadows for a polished look.

Refining Light and Shadow with Curves:

1. Add a Curves adjustment layer above your composite layers.
2. Using the Curves graph, you can adjust the overall brightness and contrast of your composite. Additionally, by creating specific curves in the graph, you can target specific tonal areas. For example, lifting a curve in the shadows can brighten them selectively, adding depth to your scene.

12.5: Real-world examples and case studies showcasing the application of advanced editing skills

In this section, we test our advanced photoshop skills on a travel photo as our case study, analysing possible tweaks that can bring such an image to life.

12.6.1 Case Study: Bringing a Travel Photo to Life

Assuming we were lucky to take the photo on the left in the collage (tagged before). It's a lovely picture, but it lacks a certain vibrancy and depth. Let's see how we can use advanced editing techniques to elevate this photo to a whole new level.

Desired Outcome: Our goal is to create a more dynamic and visually captivating image. We want to enhance the colors of the scene, add depth and realism to the water, and create a touch of drama with a subtle vignette effect.

Step-by-Step Techniques:

1. **Color Grading for Vibrancy:** We'll use a Curves adjustment layer to bring out the rich colors of the scene. By adjusting the curve, we can increase the saturation of the blue tones in the ocean, making it appear more vibrant and inviting. We can also tweak the red and yellow tones to enhance the colors of the houses on the hillside.
2. **Selective Color Adjustments:** Let's use Selective Color adjustments to fine-tune specific color ranges. We might target the greens and yellows, slightly reducing their saturation to create a more harmonious color balance within the scene.
3. **Refining the Water with Brushes:** To add depth and realism to the water, we can use custom brushes with a water texture to create subtle ripples and waves on the ocean surface. We'll use masking techniques to ensure these water texture overlays blend seamlessly with the existing water in the photograph.
4. **Vignette for Drama:** Finally, we can add a subtle vignette effect using a Curves adjustment layer with an inverted S-curve shape. This will darken the edges of the photo ever so slightly, drawing the viewer's eye towards the central focal point of the image, which is likely the charming fishing village nestled amidst the colorful houses.

By applying these techniques, you can transform your travel photo from a simple snapshot into a visually captivating image that captures the essence and vibrancy of the Italian coastline.

12.5.2 Sharpening Your Editing Eye:

As you delve deeper into the world of Photoshop 2024, honing your editing skills goes beyond mastering the technical aspects of the software. Developing a keen visual awareness is equally important. This section equips you with strategies to cultivate a critical eye for evaluating and enhancing your image edits.

Understanding the Importance of Visual Perception:

Our brains play a significant role in how we perceive images. Visual perception is influenced by factors like color, contrast, composition, and balance. A well-edited image not only adheres to technical correctness but also creates a visually pleasing and impactful experience for the viewer.

Strategies for Developing Visual Awareness:

- **Active Observation:** Train yourself to observe images critically. Pay attention to how elements are arranged, how colors interact, and how the image guides your eye. Deconstruct successful edits to understand the principles at play.
- **The Power of Reference:** Use high-quality photographs, paintings, or even well-designed advertisements as reference points. Analyze how these images employ color palettes, lighting techniques, and composition to create a visually compelling effect.
- **Embrace the Feedback Loop:** Seek constructive criticism from trusted peers or online communities. Sharing your work and receiving feedback can highlight areas for improvement and expose you to different perspectives.

Applying Visual Awareness in Photoshop:

- **Balance and Composition:** A well-composed image leads the viewer's eye through a clear visual hierarchy. Use the Rule of Thirds or leading lines to create a sense of balance and guide the viewer's attention.
- **Color Harmony and Contrast:** Colors can evoke emotions and set the mood of your image. Explore color theory to understand how complementary colors interact or how to use analogous color schemes to create a sense of harmony. Strategic use of contrast can draw attention to specific elements within your image.
- **Selective Sharpening:** Sharpening enhances edge detail, but overuse can create unwanted noise. Learn to sharpen selectively in Photoshop 2024, focusing on areas that require extra crispness without introducing artifacts.
- **The Art of Cropping:** Cropping is not just about removing unwanted elements. Use cropping strategically to enhance composition, eliminate distractions, and draw focus to the subject of your image.

Refining Your Edits Iteratively:

Developing a keen eye is an ongoing process. Train yourself to approach editing iteratively. Step away from your work periodically to come back with fresh eyes. Make small adjustments based on your evolving visual awareness and don't be afraid to experiment.

Remember:

- **Trust Your Instincts:** As you develop your visual awareness, you'll start to intuitively understand what makes an image work. Don't be afraid to trust your gut feeling when making editing decisions.

- **Practice Makes Perfect:** The more you edit and experiment, the more your visual perception will evolve. Actively engage with the editing process, and don't be discouraged by initial challenges.

By cultivating a critical eye alongside your technical skills, you'll transform from a Photoshop user into a creative image editor capable of producing visually impactful and emotionally evocative images in Photoshop 2024.

Before & After: A Powerful Tool for Visual Learning

Throughout this comprehensive guide, we've explored a vast array of editing techniques in Photoshop 2024. But how do you truly gauge the effectiveness of your edits and elevate your skills to a professional level? Enter the power of before and after analysis!

Learning from the Masters:

While analyzing your own before and after edits is valuable, take it a step further by delving into the work of professional photo editors. Many professional photographers and editing studios share before and after comparisons of their work online or in publications. Seek out these resources and use them as a powerful learning tool.

Here's how analyzing professional before and after photos can benefit you:

- **Deconstructing Expert Edits:** By comparing the 'before' image to the professional editor's 'after,' you can gain insights into their thought process and editing techniques. Did they use selective color adjustments to enhance specific tones? How did they approach cropping and composition to create a more impactful image? By dissecting their edits, you'll learn valuable strategies you can incorporate into your own workflow.
- **Identifying Industry Standards:** Professional before and after comparisons can expose you to the current trends and aesthetics in photo editing. Observe how professional editors handle common

challenges like color correction, exposure adjustments, and detail enhancement. This will help you refine your own editing skills to meet industry standards.
- **Calibrating Your Visual Perception:** Surrounding yourself with high-quality before and after edits from professionals trains your eye to recognize what constitutes a successful edit. You'll start to understand the subtle nuances of color grading, the importance of balanced composition, and the art of selective editing techniques.

Beyond Self-Evaluation:

The power of before and after analysis goes beyond personal learning. Share your own edits alongside inspiring before and after examples from professionals. This can spark discussions, generate valuable feedback, and showcase your ability to apply the techniques you've learned.

As you progress through these comparisons, pay close attention to specific edits. Ask yourself questions like:

- How did the editor use adjustment layers to achieve tonal corrections?
- What masking techniques were likely employed to isolate specific elements for selective adjustments?
- How did the color grading choices impact the mood of the final image?

By actively engaging with before-and-after analyses, you'll train your eye to identify and appreciate the subtle nuances of professional photo editing. This will not only enhance your understanding of advanced techniques but also inspire your own creative vision as you embark on your journey to becoming a master image editor.

So next time you're working on an image, take a snapshot before you begin editing. Then, actively seek out professional before and after examples. By combining your own analysis with the work of the masters, you'll transform your editing skills and develop a keen visual awareness that rivals the pros in Photoshop 2024.

12.5.3 Learning from the Masters: Pro Insights on Advanced Editing

In the final leg of our exploration, we'll gain invaluable insights from working professionals! Here, we'll have the opportunity to learn from the creative processes and thought processes behind the advanced editing choices employed by successful photographers and image editors.

Behind the Scenes with the Pros:

Imagine video interviews or written testimonials from established photographers or graphic designers. They might share:

- **Workflow Preferences:** Some professionals might favor non-destructive editing techniques using adjustment layers, while others might showcase their mastery of traditional tools and blending modes.
- **Approach to Color Grading:** Insights into how working professionals approach color grading can be incredibly valuable. They might discuss their thought processes behind choosing specific color palettes or techniques to achieve a desired mood or style.
- **Conquering Complex Compositing Challenges:** For compositing enthusiasts, learning from professionals who create fantastical scenes or seamlessly integrate 3D elements will be a treasure trove of valuable knowledge.

By gaining exposure to the creative approaches of successful artists, you'll broaden your perspective on advanced editing techniques. You'll see how these techniques are applied in real-world scenarios and gain inspiration to develop your own unique style and workflow.

Empowered to Create:

Remember, there's no single "right" way to approach advanced editing. Experimentation and exploration are key to developing your own artistic voice. The knowledge and insights gleaned from working professionals will equip you with a strong foundation and a wealth of creative possibilities as you embark on your journey to mastering photo editing.

Summary

This chapter propelled you into the realm of advanced editing, equipping you to craft captivating and impactful images. Here's a look at your newfound skills:

- **Healing and Cloning Mastery:** You conquered unwanted elements and imperfections with the Patch Tool and Content Aware capabilities of the Spot Healing Brush.
- **Crafting Flawless Composites:** You explored advanced techniques for creating realistic lighting effects, seamlessly integrating 3D elements, and achieving dynamic motion blur within your composites.
- **Precise Control with Masking:** You revisited blending modes, unlocking their creative potential when combined with adjustment layers. Nested masking workflows were unveiled, offering you the power to meticulously control how elements interact and blend within your compositions.
- **Color Grading for Impact:** You learned the art of color grading, wielding it to set the mood and evoke emotions within your viewers.
- **Professional Inspiration:** Through analyzing professional work, you gained valuable insights into how advanced techniques are applied in real-world scenarios, inspiring your own creative vision.

With these advanced techniques at your disposal, you can now create professional-looking composites, manipulate light and shadow with precision, and add depth and emotion to your images through color grading. Remember, experimentation is key to developing your unique artistic voice. This chapter has equipped you with the foundation to become a master image editor – go forth and create!

Review Questions

1. Describe two advanced cloning or healing techniques covered in this chapter and explain how they can be used to enhance an image.
2. Beyond basic blending modes, how can adjustment layers be creatively used in conjunction with them to achieve specific effects within a composite image?
3. When working on a composite image, what is the purpose of using nested masks, and how can they provide more control over the final outcome?

Conclusion: Beyond the Pixels of Photoshop 2024

Congratulations! You've reached the end of this comprehensive guide to mastering Photoshop 2024. Throughout this journey, we've explored a vast arsenal of tools and techniques, from fundamental navigation to the cutting-edge functionalities powered by artificial intelligence. But remember, this book is just the beginning. Photoshop is a boundless creative canvas, and your artistic exploration has only just commenced.

As you move forward, here are some key takeaways to empower your creative journey:

- **Embrace the Power of Practice:** Mastery takes time and dedication. Don't be discouraged by initial challenges. The more you experiment and practice, the more comfortable you'll become with Photoshop's functionalities, and the more your unique editing style will emerge.

- **Seek Inspiration and Feedback:** Immerse yourself in the work of inspiring photographers and graphic designers. Online communities and social media platforms are treasure troves of artistic expression. Don't be afraid to share your work and solicit constructive feedback – it can be an invaluable learning tool.
- **Never Stop Learning:** The world of digital art and photo editing is constantly evolving. Embrace new technologies, explore online tutorials, and stay updated with the latest trends. Photoshop itself is frequently updated with new features and functionalities. Staying curious and keeping up with these advancements will ensure you're always working at the forefront of creative expression.
- **Find Your Artistic Voice:** Don't be afraid to experiment and break away from the mold. Develop your own unique editing style that reflects your vision and artistic sensibilities. There's no single "correct" way to edit a photo – let your creativity guide you.
- **Embrace the Joy of Creation:** Above all, remember to find joy in the creative process. Photoshop is a powerful tool, but it's the human touch, your vision and emotions, that will truly elevate your edits and transform them into captivating works of art.

We hope this book has served as a valuable companion on your path to mastering Photoshop 2024. Remember, the key to unlocking your creative potential lies within you. With dedication, perseverance, and a dash of passion, you'll transform yourself from a Photoshop user into a skilled image editor, capable of crafting visually stunning and emotionally evocative works of art.

So, keep exploring, keep creating, and keep pushing the boundaries of your artistic expression. The world of visual storytelling awaits your unique perspective!

INDEX

3

3D Integration, 112, 172

A

A Creative Powerhouse at Your Fingertips, 10
A Gateway to Advanced Compositing, 178
A Glance Through Your Creative Canvas, 11, 13
A Glimpse into the Future, 8, 136
A Guide to Artistic Exploration, 57
A Legacy of Innovation, 1, 13
A Speedy Selection for Uniform Colors, 47
A Stepping Stone to Creative Exploration, 12
Accessing Generative Fill, 7
Accessing Selection Tools, 152
Accessing the Neural Filters Gallery, 57, 60
Accessing Tools in Photoshop 2024, 16
Accessing Your Recorded Action, 96
Achieving Flawless Precision, 46
Adding Pauses and Dialog Boxes, 97
Adding Realism, 160
Adjust brush size and settings (Optional), 156
Adjusting Layer Opacity, 151
Adjustment Layers for Shadows and Highlights, 160
Advanced Blending Modes, 150, 176
Advanced Cloning and Healing, 170
Advanced Compositing Workflows, 171
Advanced Cropping and Transformation Techniques, 20
Advanced Skin Tone Correction and Color Balancing, 84
Advanced Techniques for Eyes and Teeth, 158
AI Analyzes and Generates Suggestions, 127
AI for Initial Object Selection, 51
AI in Image Editing Landscape, 31
AI Integration, 9, 10, 104, 109, 128
AI to the Rescue, 49
AI-assisted Content Generation, 132
AI-powered Accessibility Checks, 133
AI-powered Background Removal, 131
AI-powered Content Optimization, 129
AI-powered Design for Responsive Layouts, 135
AI-powered Melodies and Soundscapes, 68
AI-powered Selection Tools, 38
AI-powered Skin Smoothing and Blemish Removal, 83
Applying a Style Transfer Effect, 60
Applying Visual Awareness in Photoshop, 183
Aspect Ratio Constrain, 21
Avoiding Misrepresentation and False Advertising, 88

B

Background Layer, 24
Background Removal with AI, 50
Background Segmentation, 45
Batch Editing Made Easy, 161
Behind the Scenes with the Pros, 186
Benefits of AI-powered Features, 32
Beyond Basic Adjustments, 26
Beyond Blending Modes, 171
Beyond the Basics, 25
Boosting Workflow and Efficiency, 5
Breathing New Life into Old Photos with Style Transfer, 60
Bringing Still Elements to Life, 175
Bringing the Extraordinary to Life, 172
Brush over the imperfection, 156
Brush Tool Adjustments, 81, 86
Brush Tool" with an adjustment layer in "Overlay" blending mode, 86

C

Canvas and Image Information, 141
Capturing Dialog Boxes, 97
Channel Masking Magic, 170
Channel Targeting in Action, 167
Choosing a Task, 102
Clean Product Cutouts for E-commerce Success, 50
Color Balance, 27, 29, 85, 89, 172, 177, 179
Color Grading, 10, 61, 158, 178, 179, 181, 186, 187
Color Profiles, 27
Color Range Selections, 169
Color Range Selections in Action, 169
Color Transfer, 58, 59, 61, 62, 63
Combining AI and Traditional Methods, 48
Constructing a Custom Script that Utilizes AI Functionalities, 104
Content editing and proofreading, 67
Content production, 69
Content-Aware Cropping, 20
Content-Aware Fill, 5, 8, 32, 39, 155, 156
Content-Aware Fill and Healing Brush, 39
Context-aware Design Variations, 129
Continuous Innovation and The Future (2000s-Present), 4
Convolutional Neural Networks (CNNs), 35
Create video content, 67
Creating a Script that Calls an External AI Library to Enhance Image Editing Tasks, 105
Creating an AR Experience for E-commerce Packaging, 118
Creating an AR Experience for Magazine Advertisements, 119
Creating an AR Experience for Museum Exhibits, 118
Creating Depth with Lighting, 172
Creating Nested Masks for Realistic Flower Overlap, 178
Cropping Tool, 16
Customizable Workspace, 8
Customizing Filter Effects (Optional), 59
Customizing Keyboard Shortcuts, 144

D

Data Quality and Quantity, 36
Deep Dive into AI-powered Skin Retouching, 76
Democratizing Content Creation, 69
Depth Effects, 58
Development Environment Setup, 106
Different Types of Neural Networks in Photoshop, 35
Docking and Arranging Panels, 143
Dodge and Burn, 12, 157, 166, 179
Dodge and Burn for Precise Light and Shadow Control, 157
Dreamy Landscape Composite, 163
Drop Shadows, 160

E

Early Days and Pixel-Pioneering Efforts (1980s), 3
Effectively Utilizing the Toolbar, 149
Efficiency and Time-Saving Benefits, 69
Efficiency Boosters, 23
Effortless Portrait Selection with AI, 49
Emerging AI Technologies for Design, 133
Empowered to Create, 187
Empowering new creators, 70
Enhancing Adaptive Design with AI, 135
Essential Tools for Everyday Editing, 12
Ethical Considerations and Responsible Use of AI, 133
Ethical Considerations of AI, 40
Evolving Consumer Expectations, 70
Exploring AI Tools for Design Automation, 131
Exploring Blend Mode Options, 166
Exploring New and Revamped Tools, 145
Exploring the Filter Categories and Previews, 57
Eye Widening (Optional), 168

F

Feathering and Anti-aliasing, 23
Filter Categories, 57, 58
Free Transform (Ctrl/Cmd + T), 22
Frequency Separation Mastery, 165
Frequency Separation with Skin Smoothing, 85
From Static to Immersive, 120

G

Gradient Masks, 154

H

Harnessing the Creative Potential of Neural Filters, 56, 57
Healing Brush, 12, 39, 83, 84, 87, 89, 155, 156, 157, 170, 171, 187
Here are some additional tips for utilizing AI-powered layout suggestions effectively, 128
Here are some additional tips to stay ahead of the curve and harness the potential of 3D and AR for creative expression, 123
Here are some steps to consider when incorporating 3D and AR into your storytelling, 122
Here's a breakdown of how AI-powered layout suggestions work in Photoshop 2024, 126
Here's a breakdown of the key components of a neural network, 34
Here's a glimpse into some popular blending modes and their applications, 151
Here's how to get started with incorporating 3D and AR into your design presentations, 121
High Pass Filter, 79, 86
High-Fashion Editorial Retouching, 162
High-Pass Filter Finesse, 165
Hitting the Green Button, 99
How Neural Networks Learn, 35
Hue/Saturation Adjustment, 26, 29

Human Expertise Still Matters, 33

I

Identify tasks well-suited for AI, 89
Identifying Tasks Well-Suited for AI Assistance, 78
Impact on Human Creativity, 72
Importing and Positioning Your 3D Model, 173
Interactive design presentations, 114
Isolating Objects with Precision, 45

J

JavaScript, 92, 101, 103, 105, 106, 109
Joint Ownership, 71

K

Keeping It Neat, 144

L

Landscape Mixer, 58, 59, 61, 63
Lasso Tool, 17, 43, 45, 47, 48, 49, 50, 52, 54, 152
Lasso Tool (Freehand Selection), 17
Layer Blending Modes, 53, 160
Layer Opacity and Blending Mode, 24
Learning Resources, 103
Lens Blur (Camera Raw), 146
Lens Blur panel, 147
Let's delve into some potential AI-powered design automation tools within Photoshop 2024, 131
Let's explore some sculpting techniques for common areas, 168
Leveraging AI for Interactive AR, 111
Leveraging AI-powered Filters and Adjustments in Photoshop 2024, 79
Leveraging Color and Tone, 47
Leveraging Layers for Non-Destructive Editing, 24
Limitations of AI in Photoshop, 33
Link AR elements in the AR Authoring Tool, 118, 119, 120

Liquify Responsibly, **168**
Locating the Actions Panel, **93**

M

Magic Wand Tool, **47**, **48**, **54**
Maintain design consistency, **128**
Maintaining Artistic Control, **82**
Maintaining Authenticity and Transparency, **87**
Marquee Tools (Rectangular, Elliptical, etc.), **152**
Masking Magic with a Bird in Flight, **174**
Masking Techniques, **81**, **154**, **169**
Mastering Blending Modes, **25**
Mastering Core Toolbar Tools (Not affected by new features), **149**
Mastering Nested Masks Opens Doors, **174**
Mastering the Art of AI-Driven Retouching, **76**
Matching Lighting and Color, **160**
Matching Lighting with Adjustment Layers, **172**
Material Magic and Lighting Control, **173**
Mitigating Algorithmic Bias in AI Content Creation, **72**
Mixer Brush Magic, **167**
Modifying Action Steps, **97**
Monitor Calibration, **27**

N

Navigating the Workspace in Photoshop 2024, **140**
Nested Masking Mastery, **177**
Nested Masking Workflows, **174**
Network Architecture, **33**, **37**
New Layers, **24**
Noise Reduction, **39**, **78**
Noise Reduction and Sharpening, **39**
Non-Destructive Editing with Layers and Adjustment Layers, **150**

O

Object Selection Tool (AI-powered), **152**
Object-Aware Adjustments with Select Subject, **80**
Optimizing Design Workflows with AI Automation, **136**
Option Bar (Top), **143**
Ownership by Developers, **71**

P

Parametric Filters (Beta), **148**
Patch Tool Perfection, **171**
Pen Tool (Precise Path Selection), **19**
Performing the Task, **102**
Personalized User Interface (UI) Design, **133**
Personalizing Your Workspace for Efficiency, **143**
Perspective Adjustments, **160**
Portrait Sculpting with Liquify, **168**
Predictive Editing and Recommendations, **40**
Preserving Natural Skin Texture with AI, **85**
Product visualization, **113**

Q

Quick Selection Tool, **43**, **47**, **48**, **54**

R

Real-World Applications of New Features, **8**
Recording the Script, **102**
Recording Your Action, **94**
Refinement for Perfection, **49**, **52**
Refining and Customizing AI-generated Results in Photoshop 2024, **81**
Refining Control with Advanced Masking, **173**
Refining Light and Shadow with Curves, **180**
Refining the Water with Brushes, **181**
Refining Your Edits Iteratively, **183**
Respecting Individuality and Diversity, **88**

Responsible and Ethical Use of AI in Design, 137
Revealing Smoothing Effect, 82
Running the Script, 103

S

Saving the Script, 102
Saving Your Customized Workspace, 144
Scripting Fundamentals, 101
Scripts vs. Actions, 92
Seamless Compositing with AI and Traditional Techniques, 51
Selection Tools Revisited, 17
Selective Adjustments, 78, 80, 82, 87, 152, 153
Selective Color, 17, 26, 28, 78, 80, 82, 84, 89, 158, 179, 181
Setting Up Batch Processing, 99
Sharpening, 40, 161, 182, 183
Simulating Motion Blur with a Speeding Car, 175
Skin Retouching, 78, 79, 80, 82, 86, 157
Skin Smoothing Filter, 83
Smart Object Manipulation with AI, 132
Spot Healing Brush with AI, 83
Strategies for Developing Visual Awareness, 182
Symbiosis in Action, 10
Symbiosis of Tradition and Innovation, 13
System Requirements and Hardware Acceleration, 40

T

Targeted Adjustments for Natural Enhancement, 168
Testing and Refining, 97
Testing in Photoshop, 108
The Batch Processing Powerhouse, 98
The Benefits of Automation, 93
The Foundation of Your Workflow, 9
The Language of Efficiency, 162
The potential applications of AR are vast and constantly, 113
The Power of AI-powered Identification, 45
The Power of Synergy, 48
The Rise of a Creative Powerhouse (1990s-Early 2000s), 3
The Takeaway, 11
There are several factors that influence the effectiveness of training a neural network, 36
Throughout this chapter, we'll embark on a fascinating exploration, 1
To use Generative Fill, 7
To use Smart Filters and Effects, 6
Tonal Adjustments, 178, 179
Tool Options and Contextual Menus, 149
Tool Shortcuts, 162
Traditional Editing Tools, 9
Traditional Selection Methods, 46
Traditional Tools for Final Touches, 51
Traditional Tools for Integration and Refinement, 52
Train the AI in Photoshop, 118, 119
Training Parameters, 37
Transformation Techniques, 28
Transformation Tools, 16
Transforming Design and Narrative, 111
Transforming Landscapes, 61

U

Understanding AI-powered user behavior analysis, 130
Understanding Color Space, 27
Understanding Layer Hierarchy, 24
Understanding Neural Networks, 34
Understanding Scripting Languages, 100
Understanding Scripts, 92, 102
Understanding the Fundamentals of Compositing, 159
Understanding the Importance of Visual Perception, 182
Understanding the Interface Components, 142
Understanding the Layout, 11
Understanding the Power of AI, 57

Understanding the Toolbar, **145**
Unleash the Power of AI for Interactive AR, **115**
Unlocking Creative Potential with Adjustment Layers, **177**
Unveiling the Magic of AI-powered Layout Suggestions, 126
Unveiling the Power of 2024, **2, 5, 13**
Unveiling the Power of AI Writing Assistants, 66
Unveiling the Power of Individual Filters, 58
User-Centered Design Informed by AI Analytics, **136**
Utilize user-friendly AR creation tools, **122**
Utilizing Adjustment Layers for Selective Edits, **153**
Utilizing AI insights to inform user-centered design decisions, **130**

Vignette for Drama, **181**

What is AI, 31
What is Generative Fill, **6**
Who Owns AI-Generated Content?, 71